Nick Vandom

A Parent's Guide to the iPad

in
easy steps

3rd edition

covers iOS 7

for iPad 2 – 5 (iPad Air) and iPad Mini

In easy steps is an imprint of In Easy Steps Limited
16 Hamilton Terrace · Holly Walk · Leamington Spa
Warwickshire · United Kingdom · CV32 4LY
www.ineasysteps.com

Third Edition

Notice of Liability
Every effort has been made to ensure that this book contains accurate
and current information. However, In Easy Steps Limited and the
author shall not be liable for any loss or damage suffered by readers
as a result of any information contained herein.

Trademarks
All trademarks are acknowledged as belonging to their respective
companies.

In Easy Steps Limited supports The Forest Stewardship Council (FSC),
the leading international forest certification organisation. All our titles
that are printed on Greenpeace approved FSC certified paper carry the
FSC logo.

MIX
Paper from
responsible sources
FSC® C020837

Printed and bound in the United Kingdom

ISBN 978-1-84078-611-8

Contents

6   iPad for Productivity   109

7   Photos and Videos   151

1 Your Child Needs an iPad

For a parent, the thought of your child having an iPad can be a daunting one. Will they look after it? Will they use it productively? Will they be safe? This chapter introduces giving an iPad to your child and shows how to use it effectively.

The iPad Revolution

Apple Computers has the happy knack of turning the way we look at the world of computing on its head. The first, most dramatic example of this was the introduction of the iMac: an all-in-one desktop computer that was so stylish that people wanted to have it on display rather than hide it away in a study or a spare bedroom. This was followed by the iBook and the MacBook: laptops that quickly featured in a range of hip and savvy television programs and films. But the two products that propelled Apple into the real mainstream of consumer electronics were the iPod and the iPhone. The iPod quickly became the number one MP3 device for playing digital music and the iPhone followed by taking the smartphone market by storm. The iPod and the iPhone ensured that Apple was no longer simply viewed as a manufacturer of computers, albeit very iconic ones.

The i What?

Following on from the success of its other i devices, Apple introduced the first iPad in January 2010. Initially, sceptics scratched their heads in a rather puzzled fashion: what was the iPad exactly? It seemed to lack the productivity to replace a traditional laptop and it was too large to be just a communications device. But, as is their habit, Apple had launched the right product at exactly the right time. The iPad is a tablet computer that is compact, has a longer battery life than a laptop and has a range of functionality for both work and entertainment. Because of its size, it is easily carried in a bag, or even a large pocket, and has Wi-Fi and, in some versions, 3G/4G connectivity to the Web. And of course the design has the usual Apple wow-factor and immediately makes people want to have one as soon as they see it. This, added to a number of celebrity endorsements, has ensured that, with the iPad, the era of the tablet computer has well and truly arrived.

Don't forget

There is a range of models for the iPad, including the latest ones, the iPad Air and the iPad Mini, both with a Retina Display. All iPads from the iPad 2 onwards can use iOS 7, the latest version of Apple's mobile operating system.

A Perfect Match

For adults, who have grown up with the evolution of the desktop PC, the iPad can initially seem like something of a strange beast – it is almost too good at what it does; being able to handle most computing tasks while still being stylish and compact. But for children it is a perfect match. Untainted by the times when computers only came in beige boxes, today's children are used to mobile computing devices that let them communicate, study and play in as easy a way as possible. In this respect the iPad ticks all of the boxes. Also, being a style icon does no harm in terms of its appeal to children.

Some of the areas in which the iPad is ideal for children are:

Beware

iPads are not inexpensive so safeguards should be taken to prevent them being lost or stolen from you child. See Chapter Three for more information about physical security.

- **Appearance.** In an era where brand is more important than ever before, the name Apple is one of the most recognizable among children. The iPad is seen as something that children are more than happy to show to their peers and, rather than being seen as a dull computer, it is much sought-after, partly because of its stylish appearance and its brand appeal.

- **Battery life.** Children have busy, active lives and they do not want to have to worry about constantly charging their mobile devices. With a battery life of up to 10 hours, the iPad ensures that frustration with recharging is kept to a minimum.

- **Size.** The iPad is compact enough to be put in a jacket or a school bag and big enough to be used effectively for most computing tasks.

- **Apps.** The iPad comes with a range of its own apps (programs) and there are thousands more that can be downloaded from the App Store. These cover everything from entertainment to education. Some of them are free while others have to be paid for. But there will almost certainly be an app for whatever interests your child.

Using an iPad

Any parent, grandparent or teacher who is responsible for a child using an iPad will want to know exactly what can be done with it. Because of its versatile nature this may depend on the child's creativity and inventiveness, but the using the iPad can be broken down into two main categories:

● Using iPad apps

● Using App Store apps

iPad apps

iPad apps are those that come pre-installed with the iPad. These can be accessed from the icons on the iPad Home screen:

● **App Store.** This can be used to access the App Store, from where additional apps can then be downloaded.

● **Calendar.** An app for storing appointments, important dates and other calendar information. It can be synced with iCloud.

● **Clock.** This can be used to view the time in different countries and also as an alarm clock and a stopwatch.

● **Contacts.** An address book app. Once contacts are added here they can then also be accessed from other apps, such as Mail.

Hot tip

If your iPad ever freezes, or if something is not working properly, it can be re-booted by holding down the **Home** and **On/Off** button for 10 seconds and then turning it on again (see Chapter Two, page 24 for details of the controls on the iPad).

Hot tip

To download apps from the App Store, the user will need an Apple ID. Since some apps have to be paid for, it is best if this is set up, and administered, by an adult rather than give control of it to a child. See page 21 for details about obtaining an Apple ID.

- **FaceTime.** This is an app that uses the built-in FaceTime camera on the iPad to hold video chats with other iPad users, or those with an iPhone, iPod Touch or a Mac computer.

- **Game Center.** For those who like gaming, this is an app for playing a variety of games, either individually or with friends.

- **iBooks.** This is an app for downloading electronic books, that can then be read on the iPad. This can be done for plain text or illustrated iBooks. Although this is considered a built-in app, it has to be downloaded from the App Store first.

- **iTunes Store.** This app can be used to browse the iTunes store where music, TV shows, movies and more, can be downloaded to your iPad.

- **Mail.** This is the email app for sending and receiving email on your iPad.

- **Maps.** Use this app to view maps from around the world, find specific locations and get directions to destinations:

- **Messages.** This is the iPad messaging service, that can be used between iPads, iPhones, iPod Touches and Mac computers. It can be used with not only text but also photos and videos.

To use FaceTime the other user must have iOS 5, or later, on their iPad, iPhone or iPod Touch or OS X Lion (7.2 or later) on their Mac.

Items in apps including Calendar, FaceTime, Game Center, Mail, Messages and Reminders can be flagged up in the Notification Center. This is accessed by dragging downwards from the top of the iPad screen.

11

...cont'd

● **Music.** An app for playing music on your iPad and also for viewing cover artwork. You can also use it to create your own playlists.

● **Newsstand.** Similar to iBooks, this app can be used to download and read newspaper and magazine subscriptions.

● **Notes.** If you need to jot down your thoughts or ideas, this app is just perfect for that.

● **Photo Booth.** A photography app that can be used to create distorted and special effects photos of people or objects:

● **Photos.** This is an app for viewing and editing photos and creating slideshows.

● **Reminders.** Use this app for organization, when you want to create to-do lists and set reminders for events.

● **Safari.** The Apple web browser that has been developed for viewing the Web on your iPad.

● **Videos.** This is an app for viewing videos on your iPad and also streaming them to a larger HDTV monitor.

Using an iPad Together

Once your child has an iPad there will be many occasions when they will want to use it on their own, for either studying, playing games or communicating with their friends. However, you should try to ensure that it is not solely a solitary pastime; try to develop the feeling that using the iPad can also be a shared experience. This can help you understand how your child is using the iPad and you can also discuss any potential problems. Talk openly about what you expect the iPad to be used for and aim to create mutual trust about a balance between using it as

a study tool and also an entertainment center. But most of all, try to make sure that you and your child can make using the iPad together an enjoyable experience.

When you are using the iPad with your child there are some areas you should think about:

- Offer support and help when needed but be prepared to take a back seat if your child is coping well without your help. Try not to take over, even if you think you know best.

- Be prepared to learn yourself. It is sometimes a hard fact to accept, but there are times when our children know more than we do! So look forward to learning new skills and embrace the chance to let your child teach you.

- Talk openly about potential problem areas. These could include inappropriate websites and issues about talking to strangers on message boards. If you can talk honestly about these things then your child is more likely to come to you if there is a problem.

Hot tip

Try to find a shared interest with your child on the iPad, such as a hobby you can research, or a game you can play together and compare your scores.

13

An Education Tool

In terms of exactly what an iPad should be used for, there may be some divergence of opinion between parents and their offspring, with the former championing it as an education tool and the latter favoring it as a games and communications device. However, the good news is that the education elements of the iPad can be a lot of fun in themselves, so a happy compromise should be easy to achieve. There are two ways in which the iPad can be used as an education tool:

- **Productivity apps.** These are apps that can be used for producing, saving, sharing and printing school work

- **Learning apps.** These are education apps that can be used for learning for all ages

Productivity apps

The three main apps for this are:

- **Pages**, for word processing

- **Numbers**, for spreadsheets and databases

- **Keynote**, for presentations

These apps can be downloaded from the App Store and files can also be saved into formats compatible with Microsoft Office apps, Word, Excel and PowerPoint.

Pages, Numbers and Keynote have to be paid for, but they are less expensive than their Microsoft Office counterparts.

For more information about using productivity apps, see Chapter Six.

Learning Apps

Learning apps can be downloaded from the App Store and there is a huge range of them, covering all age groups.

Pre-school children are catered for with early-learning apps covering reading, writing and counting.

For older children there are apps for all of the main subjects that are likely to be studied at school.

Hot tip

Languages are covered in the Education category within the App Store and there are flashcards for several languages including French, Spanish, Chinese, Korean and Indonesian.

An Entertainment Tool

When a child picks up an iPad their first port of call may not be an app to do their English or science homework (but hopefully this will come later). Instead they are more likely to focus on the entertainment functions available. These fall broadly into two categories:

- **Media.** Apps for accessing photos, music and videos

- **Games.** There are thousands of games apps that can be downloaded from the App Store – these can be played independently, or through the Game Center app

Media

For viewing and editing music, photos and video, the apps with the same name can be used. These apps can display graphical covers when playing music and create artistic slideshows for viewing photos.

Apps such as iTunes and Photos can also be used to download music from the iTunes Store and edit photos respectively.

Hot tip

You can connect an iPad to a large screen HD television for viewing videos or photos. This is done by attaching an Apple Digital AV Adapter (Lightning or 30-pin connector), which is sold separately.

Don't forget

For more information about using photo, music and video apps, see Chapters Seven and Eight.

Game Center

The pre-installed Game Center app enables you to play a range of games, either by yourself or with like-minded people with an iPad, iPhone or iPod Touch. This will link to a game-playing network where you can compare scores against individuals or join a multiplayer game.

For more information about using games apps, see Chapter Eight.

App Store Games

The App Store has a range of games for all tastes and ages. Browse through them on the Games category page or type in a keyword in the search box to find a specific game.

Within the Games category of the App Store there are sections for **New This Week**, **Updated This Week**, **What We're Playing**, **What's Hot** and **Better with Game Center**.

17

A Window to the World

No computer, or mobile device, is complete without access to the Internet and the Web. On the iPad this is provided by the Safari web browser app. This provides standard access to the Web, but with one main difference for the traditional computer user.

What, no mouse?

The iPad has no mouse, something that may confuse users from the generation that grew up with this ubiquitous pointing device. However, times move on and the navigation on the iPad is done by a collection of taps, swipes and pinching gestures. These are know as Multi-Touch Gestures and they are used to navigate web pages within Safari. Two of the main areas are:

Scrolling

To move up and down web pages, swipe in the opposite direction to the one in which you want the page to move:

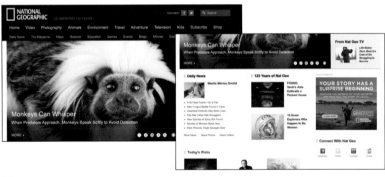

Zooming

To zoom in on an item on a web page, spread outwards with thumb and forefinger (or double-tap with one finger):

Don't forget

All of the navigation on an iPad is done with Multi-Touch Gestures and these are looked at in detail in Chapter Two.

Beware

Multi-Touch Gestures can take a bit of getting used to, so don't panic if you cannot get the hang of them immediately. However, children tend to take to them with more ease.

Communicating with an iPad

The younger generation live in a world in which they expect to be fully connected with their friends in a range of digital ways: phone, text, email, messaging (text and video) and social networking. The iPad caters for most of these needs so that your child is only ever a click away from their friends.

Mail

This is the email app on the iPad. An account can be set up with the free Apple iCloud service or settings for an existing account can be added.

Sometimes you can get too much of a good thing and so some forms of communications by your child may need to be monitored. This can include messaging and social networking in particular.

When receiving email, attachments can be viewed directly within mail without having to open them separately.

For more information about using Safari and Mail on the iPad, see Chapter Nine.

...cont'd

Text messages in Messages are typed with the virtual keyboard that appears when you are ready to create a new text message.

For more information about using Messages and FaceTime on the iPad, see Chapter Nine.

iMessages

This is the text messaging service on the iPad that can be used for free with other iPad, iPhone, iPod Touch and Mac (with OS X Mountain Lion or later) users. It works with the Messages app, over Wi-Fi or 3G/4G networks, and messages can also include photos and videos that you have on your iPad.

Conversations can be held with individual people:

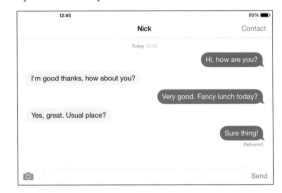

FaceTime

FaceTime is an app that enables you to make video calls over Wi-Fi or 3G/4G networks with other iPad, iPhone, iPod Touch or Mac computer users. You have to sign in with an Apple ID (see next page) and an email address and once you have done this you can then make video calls:

The FaceTime camera is the one facing you when you are looking at the screen. The other camera on the iPad cannot be used for FaceTime calls.

Obtaining an Apple ID

An Apple ID is a registered email address and password with Apple that enables you to log in and use a variety of Apple services. These include:

- App Store

- iTunes Store

- iCloud (for backing up your content and sharing it on other iCloud-enabled devices. See Chapter Ten for more details)

- iMessage

- FaceTime

- Game Center

- iBooks

It is free to register for an Apple ID and this can be done when you access one of the apps or services which requires this, or you can do it on the Apple website at My Apple ID:

If you are using an Apple ID to buy items, such as from iTunes or the App Store, you will need to provide a valid method of payment.

My Apple ID is where you can access your Apple ID details and edit them, if required.

1. Tap once on the **Create an Apple ID** button

   Create an Apple ID

2. Enter your email address and a password

   Create an Apple ID.

   Choose an Apple ID and password.
   Enter your primary email address as your Apple ID. This will be used as the contact email address for your account. Please note that this email address must be verified before you can use certain Apple services.

   Apple ID   @mac.com

   Password   ••••••••

   Confirm Password ••••••••

   Create a security question.
   Select a security question or create one of your own. This question will help us verify your identity should you forget your password.

When you register for your Apple ID you will be sent a verification email to the email address that you have provided. Follow the instructions in it to complete the registration process.

3. Enter additional details such as date of birth and address. Enter the security code and tap once on the **Create Apple ID** button

   Please type the characters you see in the image below.

   QCTGR

   ↻ Try a different image
   ◀) Vision Impaired

   QCTGR
   Letters are not case sensitive.

   ☑ I have read and agree to the Apple Terms of Service and Apple Customer Privacy Policy.

   Cancel   Create Apple ID

Security Overview

There is almost no limit to the ways in which an iPad can be used for education, entertainment and communication. However, for any parent, grandparent or teacher, one of the main concerns will be security. This falls into two main categories:

- **Physical security.** This covers ensuring, as much as possible, that your child's iPad is not lost or stolen

- **iPad security.** This covers what can, and cannot, be done on the iPad and the Web

For an in-depth look at security and restrictions, see Chapter Three.

Physical security

Some areas to bear in mind once your child has an iPad are:

- **Where is it going to be used?** If the iPad is only going to be used in the home then this represents less of a security risk. However, if it is going to be taken to different places then some consideration should be taken about how to keep it safe

- **If it is being carried around is it inconspicuous?** Since an iPad is a small, and valuable, item it can be an easy target for anyone trying to steal it. Therefore it is advisable to keep it out of view when it is being carried around

- **Is it insured?** Insurance can be obtained for an iPad when you buy it or it may be covered by household insurance. However, check any policies carefully to ensure that they provide sufficient cover

iPad security

Within the **Settings** app of the iPad are a number of restrictions that can be applied to a range of apps and content:

ALLOWED CONTENT:	
Ratings For	United States >
Music, Podcasts & iTunes U	Explicit >
Movies	All >
TV Shows	All >
Books	All >
Apps	All >
Siri	All >
Websites	All >

2 Getting to Know the iPad

Even if your child is going to be the main user of the iPad, it is still important for you to understand its functions and capabilities. This chapter takes you around the hardware and software that makes up the iPad. This includes some of the new iOS 7 features such as multitasking and using the Control Center. After getting used to the iPad, and seeing how powerful it is, you may want to use it yourself too.

Around the iPad

The controls for the iPad are simple and uncomplicated. Three of them are situated at the top of the iPad and the other is in the middle at the bottom. There are also two cameras, one on the front and one on the back of the iPad.

Controls

The controls at the top of the iPad are:

On/Off button

Side Switch for silent mode (this applies to system sounds rather than the volume of items such as music or videos)

Volume Up or **Down** button

Cameras. One is located on the back (iSight), underneath the On/Off button and one on the front top (FaceTime HD)

Home button. Press this once to wake up the iPad or return to the Home screen at any point

Speaker. The speaker is located here on the bottom of the iPad:

Lightning cable connector. Connect the dock cable here to charge the iPad, connect it to an iPad Dock, or another computer. (iPad 2 and the third generation iPad come with a 30-pin connector. See tip on page 25.)

The iPad has an iSight camera on the back, which can also capture video in HD. The other camera is a FaceTime HD camera, for use with the FaceTime app for video calls.

Press and hold the On/Off button for a few seconds to turn the iPad On or Off.

iPads do not have any USB ports or DVD/CD drives. If you want to transfer items from an iPad this generally has to be done by sending them by email, sharing them with iTunes or the online Apple service, iCloud. For more details about sharing files, see Chapter 10.

Specifications

Since its introduction, there are now several different generations of iPad, including the iPad Mini, which is smaller than the original iPad. When considering which iPad is best for your child some of the specifications to consider are:

- **Processor:** This determines the speed at which the iPad operates and how quickly tasks are performed.

- **Storage:** This determines how much content you can store on your iPad. Across the iPad family, the range of storage is 16GB, 32GB, 64GB or 128GB.

- **Connectivity:** The options for this are Wi-Fi and 3G/4G connectivity for the Internet and Bluetooth for connecting to other devices over short distances. All models of iPad have Wi-Fi connectivity as standard.

- **Screen:** Both the full size version of the latest generation of the iPad (iPad Air) and the iPad Mini have a Retina Display screen. This is a LED-backlit glossy widescreen multi-touch display with 2048 by 1536 pixel resolution.

- **Operating System**. The full size version of the iPad and the iPad Mini both run on the iOS 7 operating system. This can be used on all iPads from the iPad 2 and later.

- **Battery power:** This is the length of time the iPad can be used for general use such as surfing the Web on Wi-Fi, watching video, or listening to music. All models offer approximately 10 hours of use in this way.

- **Input/Output:** Both the iPad and the iPad Mini have similar output/input options. These are a lightning connector port (for charging), 3.5 mm stereo headphone minijack, built-in speaker, microphone and micro-SIM card tray (Wi-Fi and 4G model only).

- **Sensors:** These are used to access the amount of ambient light and also the orientation in which the iPad is being held. The sensors are accelerometer, ambient light sensor and gyroscope.

- **TV and video:** This determines how your iPad can be connected to a High Definition TV. This is done with AirPlay Mirroring.

The latest version of the full size iPad is the fifth generation of the device, known as the iPad Air.

The fourth generation (and later) iPad comes with the new lightning connector. So, you'll need to buy adapters to connect it to your "old" 30-pin accessories, such as TV, iPod dock, etc.

Lightning Connector Adapter

Lightning Connector

30-pin dock Connector

Setting Up

To start using the iPad, press the On/Off button once and hold it down for a few seconds.

Initially, there will be a series of setup screens to move through before you can use the iPad: These include the following options (a lot of these can be skipped during the setup and accessed later from the **Settings** app).

- **Language.** Select the language you want to use.

- **Country.** Select the country in which you are located.

- **Location Services.** This determines whether your iPad can use your geographical location for apps that use this type of information (such as Maps).

- **Wi-Fi network.** Select a Wi-Fi network to connect to the Internet. If you are at home, this will be your own Wi-Fi network, if available. If you are at a Wi-Fi hotspot then this will appear on your network list.

- **Apple ID.** You can register with this to be able to access a range of Apple facilities, such as iCloud, purchase items on iTunes or the App Store, Facetime, Messages and iBooks. You can also create an Apple ID whenever you access one of the relevant apps for the first time.

- **iCloud.** This is Apple's online service for sharing and backing up content. You need an Apple ID in order to use this and once it has been set up you can use it to back up your content and also share items such as notes, calendars, contacts and reminders on any other iCloud-enabled device, such as an iPhone or another Mac computer.

- **Find My iPad.** This is a service that can be activated so that you can locate your iPad if it is lost or stolen. This is done via the online iCloud site at **www.icloud.com**

- **Diagnostic information.** This enables information about your iPad to be sent to Apple.

- **Register.** This enables you to register your iPad with Apple, as the registered owner.

- **Start using.** Once the setup process has been completed you can start using your iPad.

Hot tip

The Find My iPad function can also be set up within the **Privacy > Location Services** and **iCloud** sections of the **Settings** app.

About iOS 7

iOS 7 is the latest version of the operating system for Apple's mobile devices including the iPad, the iPhone and the iPod Touch. Some of the new features include:

New design
iOS 7 is one of the most dramatic cosmetic changes to the operating system in its history. It was overseen by the designer Jonathan Ive, who was responsible for some of the most iconic Apple devices including the iMac, iPod and iPhone. The design is intended to be a cleaner, simpler one and moves away from previous styles, which relied on the interpretation of everyday materials such as paper, leather, wood and felt.

The interpretation of everyday items in the design of computer interfaces is known as skeuomorphic.

Control Center
This is a way of quickly accessing some of the commonly used functions on the iPad. It can be activated by swiping up from the bottom of any screen.

Multitasking
Some previous versions of iOS had a Multitasking bar, but this has been redesigned in iOS 7 so that it provides a full screen option for viewing and using your open apps and also closing them.

Camera and Photos
This includes options for taking photos in different ratios, a new way of organizing and viewing your photos in the Photos app and special effects added to the editing functions.

Siri improvements
The voice assistant function that was introduced in iOS 6 has been improved further with a new interface and a wider range of content over which it can search.

To check the version of the iOS, look in **Settings > General > Software Update**.

Safari improvements
The iOS 7 web browser now has a unified Search/Address bar, an improved tabs view and shared links so that you can view your social networking updates through Safari.

First View

Once you have completed the setup process you will see the Home screen of the iPad. This contains the built-in iPad apps:

Apps can be added to, or deleted from, the Dock. See page 34 for details about this.

At the bottom of the screen are four apps that appear by default in the Dock area. Tap once on any app on the Home screen to open it:

Content on an iPad can be viewed in either portrait (vertical) or landscape (horizontal) mode. To do this, rotate the iPad and the content will be adjusted accordingly. Screen rotation can also be locked, from the Control Center, see page 33.

Home Button

The Home button, located at the bottom, middle on the iPad (in portrait mode) can be used to perform a number of tasks:

1 Click once on the **Home button** to return to the Home screen at any point

2 Double-click on the **Home button** to access the **Multitasking** window. This shows the most recently-used and open apps

Tap once on an app in the Multitasking window to open it.

3 Press and hold on the **Home button** to access the Siri voice assistant function, see pages 40-41

What can I help you with?

Multitasking Window

The Multitasking feature has been overhauled in iOS 7 and it performs a number of tasks:

● It shows open apps

● It enables you to move between open apps and access different ones

● It enables apps to be closed (see next page)

Accessing Multitasking

The Multitasking option can be accessed from any screen on your iPad, as follows:

1 Double-click on the **Home button**

The Multitasking window can also be accessed by swiping up on the screen with four fingers.

2 The currently open apps are displayed, with their icon underneath them (except the Home screen), The most recently used apps are shown first

3 Swipe left and right to view the open apps. Tap on one to access it in full screen size

Closing Items

The iPad deals with open apps very efficiently. They do not interact with other apps, which increases security and also means that they can be open in the background, without using up a significant amount of processing power, in a state of semi-hibernation until they are needed. Because of this it is not essential to close apps when you move to something else. However, you may want to close apps if you feel you have too many open or if one stops working. To do this:

1 Access the Multitasking window. The currently-open apps are displayed

2 Press and hold on an app and swipe it to the top of the screen to close it. This does not remove it from the iPad and it can be opened again in the usual way

When you switch from one app to another, the first one stays open in the background. You can go back to it by accessing it from the Multitasking window or the Home screen.

3 The app is removed from its position in the Multitasking window

Using the Control Center

The Control Center is a panel containing some of the most commonly used options within the **Settings** app. It can be accessed with one swipe and is an excellent function for when you do not want to have to go into Settings.

Accessing the Control Center

The Control Center can be accessed from any screen within iOS 7 and it can also be accessed from the Lock Screen:

1 Tap once on the **Settings** app

2 Tap once on the **Control Center** tab and drag the **Access on Lock Screen** and **Access Within Apps** buttons On or Off to specify if the Control Center can be accessed from here (if both are Off, it can still be accessed from any Home screen)

The Control Center cannot be disabled from being accessed from the Home screen.

3 Swipe up from the bottom of any screen to access the Control Center panel

4 Tap on this button to hide the Control Center panel, or tap anywhere on the screen

Control Center controls
The items that can be used in the Control Center are:

1 Use these controls for any music or video that is playing. Use the buttons to Pause/Play a track, go to the beginning or end and adjust the volume

2 Tap once on this button to turn **Airplane mode** On or Off

3 Tap once on this button to turn **Wi-Fi** On or Off

4 Tap once on this button to turn **Bluetooth** On or Off

5 Tap once on this button to turn **Do Not Disturb** mode On or Off

6 Tap once on this button to access a clock, including a stopwatch

7 Tap once on this button to open the **Camera** app

8 Use this slider to adjust the screen brightness

9 Tap once on this button to **Lock** or **Unlock** screen rotation. If it is locked the screen will not change when you change the orientation of your iPad

Hot tip

The screen rotation can also be locked from within the **General** section of the **Settings** app. Under **Use Side Switch to**, tap once on the **Lock Rotation** link. Then the side switch can be used to lock, and unlock, the screen rotation.

Items on the Dock

The apps on the Dock at the bottom of the screen can be rearranged in any way you require. The default ones are put there as it is thought they are the most commonly-used. However, you can add and remove them. To do this:

Apps can also be rearranged within the Home screen area by holding and dragging them in the same way as adding or removing them on the Dock.

1 To remove an app from the Dock, tap and hold it and drag it onto the main screen area

2 To add an app to the Dock, tap and hold it and drag it onto the Dock

Press the Home button once to save any changes to the arrangement and ordering of apps.

3 The number of items that can be added to the Dock is restricted to a maximum of six as the icons do not resize themselves

System Settings

The Settings app is the one that should probably be explored first as it controls settings for the appearance of the iPad and the way it, and its apps, operate. To use the Settings app:

1   Tap once on the **Settings** app

2   The Settings are listed down the left-hand side and the options are shown on the right-hand side

If a Settings option has an **On/Off** button next to it, this can be changed by swiping the button to either the left or right. Green indicates that the option is **On**.

35

3   Tap on a link to see additional options for that item

4   Tap once here to move back to the main category for the selected Setting

Within the Notification Center you can turn **On** or **Off** items which you want to appear there. The Notification Center is accessed by dragging downwards from the top, middle of the screen.

There are 34 Apple wallpapers and you can also select your own photos and use these.

...cont'd

The System Settings are:

- **Airplane Mode.** This can be used while on an airplane and switches off the wireless and cellular receivers

- **Wi-Fi.** This enables you to select a wireless network. Available networks will be displayed here

- **Bluetooth.** Turn this On to connect Bluetooth devices

- **Notification Center.** This determines how the Notification Center operates in terms of alerting the user to different types of notifications

- **Control Center.** This determines how the Control Center operates (see pages 32-33)

- **Do Not Disturb.** Use this to specify times when you do not want to receive audio alerts or FaceTime video calls

- **General.** This contains a number of settings for how the iPad operates. This is one of the most useful Settings

- **Sounds.** This contains options for setting sounds for alerts for items such as mail and calendar items

- **Brightness & Wallpaper.** This can be used to set the screen brightness manually or automatically and select a wallpaper

- **Privacy.** This can be used to activate Location Services so that your location can be used by specific apps

- **iCloud.** This contains settings for items that are to be saved to the online iCloud

- **Mail, Contacts, Calendars.** This has options for how these three apps operate

- **Notes.** This contains formatting options for creating items in the Notes app

- **Reminders.** This has an option for syncing your reminders for other devices, covering a period of time

- **Messages.** This can be used to sign in to the Messages app for sending and receiving text messages

- **FaceTime.** This is used to turn video calling On or Off

- **Maps.** This contains options for displaying distances in miles or kilometers in the Maps app and also the way labels are displayed on maps

- **Safari.** Settings for the Safari web browser

- **iTunes & App Store.** This can be used to specify downloading options from the iTunes Store and the App Store, for music, books and apps

- **Music.** This has options for how you listen to music

- **Videos.** This has options for how you view videos

- **Photos & Camera.** This has options for viewing and editing photos, slideshow settings and options for uploading to iCloud, using Shared Photo Streams

- **iBooks.** This contains options for reading books in the iBooks app, including hyphenation and using bookmarks

- **iTunes U.** Use this to sync your courses and notes from this online educational facility

- **Game Center.** Use this to manage your settings for allowing invitations from other players and to identify those nearby

- **Twitter.** Use this to install Twitter and create an account

- **Facebook.** As above, but for Facebook

Hot tip

When you start downloading new apps from the App Store, some of these will appear in the Settings section, if they have options that can be edited, such as using iCloud for storing items.

37

Settings for iOS 7

Details about the iOS 7 operating system can also be found within the Settings app and updates can be installed from here too. To view the iOS 7 details:

1 Tap once on the **Settings** app

Settings

2 Tap once on the **General** tab

General

Hot tip

You can change the name of the iPad in the **About** section.

3 Tap once on the **About** link

| About | > |

4 Details about the iPad are displayed. This includes information about what is stored on the iPad, its capacity and available capacity, the version of the OS, the iPad model, serial number and wireless addresses

‹ General	About	
Name		My iPad black >
Songs		211
Videos		2
Photos		747
Applications		67
Capacity		13.3 GB
Available		4.1 GB
Version		7.0 (11A465)
Model		MC705B/A
Serial Number		
Wi-Fi Address		1C:AB:A7:A4:AC:15
Bluetooth		1C:AB:A7:A4:AC:16
Diagnostics & Usage		>
Legal		>

5 Tap once on the **Software Update** link

Software Update	>

6 Details about the current version of the OS are displayed

iOS 7.0
Your software is up to date.

7 Tap once on the **Usage** link

Usage	>

8 Details about what has been stored on the iPad are displayed and also the available iCloud storage

‹ General	**Usage**	
STORAGE		
3.8 GB Available		9.5 GB Used
A & P		1.5 GB >
Music		1.2 GB >
iBooks		1.2 GB >
Keynote		540 MB >
Photos & Camera		512 MB >
Human Body		390 MB >
Scrap It HD		380 MB >
Pages		374 MB >
Numbers		369 MB >
Escapes		218 MB >
Show all Apps		
ICLOUD		
Total Storage		5.0 GB
Available		3.1 GB

Finding Things with Siri

Siri is the iPad voice assistant that provides answers to a variety of questions by looking at your iPad and also web services. You can ask Siri questions relating to the apps on your iPad and also general questions, such as weather conditions around the world, or sports results. Initially, Siri can be set up within the Settings app:

Hot tip

Using explicit language with Siri can be blocked within **Restrictions** in the **General** section of the **Settings** app. See Chapter Three for more details about setting restrictions.

1 In the General section, tap once on the **Siri** link

2 Drag the Siri button to **On** to activate the Siri functionality. Tap once on these links to select a language, set voice feedback and allow access to your details

Questioning Siri

Once you have set up Siri, you can start putting it to work with your queries. To do this:

Hot tip

Siri can be used to open any of the built-in iPad apps, simply by saying, **Open Photos**.

1 Hold down the **Home button** until the Siri window appears

2 To find something from your iPad apps, ask a question, such as **Show me my reminders**

Siri can also find information from across the Web and related web services:

1 Siri can provide sports results, for certain sports in certain countries, such as in response to the question **Show me the last three scores for Barcelona**

2 Weather reports are another of Siri's strong points and it can provide weekly forecasts in response to the question, such as **What is the weather like in Tokyo?**

Siri has a certain amount of personality and can add its own editorial comments to certain types of queries.

3 However, even Siri's knowledge is limited it will bring back information from the Web, or Wikipedia

The iPad Keyboard

The keyboard on the iPad is a virtual one, i.e. it appears on the touchscreen whenever text or numbered input is required for an app. Settings for the keyboard can be determined in the General section of the Settings app. To do this:

Don't forget

The keyboard appears automatically whenever you tap on an item to perform any input task, such as word processing, emailing, entering a web address or entering details in an online form.

1 Tap once on the **Settings** app

2 Tap once on the **General** tab

3 Tap once on the **Keyboard** link

Hot tip

To delete a shortcut, tap once on the **Edit** button at the top of the **Keyboard** window and tap once on the red circle with the minus sign inside next to a shortcut to delete it.

4 Drag the sliders to **On** or **Off** to enable or disable the relevant functions

5 Shortcuts can be created for words and phrases. To do this, click on the **Add New Shortcut** link

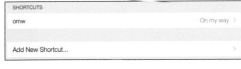

6 Enter the phrase and shortcut and tap once on the **Save** button

Undocking the keyboard

By default, the keyboard is docked at the bottom of the screen. However, it is possible to undock it so that it appears higher up the screen. To do this:

1 Press and hold on this button on the keyboard

2 Tap once on the **Undock** button

3 Drag on the button in Step 1 to move the keyboard around the screen

Splitting the keyboard

The keyboard can also be split into two and used on either side of the screen. To do this:

1 Press and hold on this button on the keyboard

2 Tap once on the **Split** button

3 The split keyboard can be moved around the screen in the same way as undocking it, by clicking on the button in Step 1

Hot tip

The button for undocking and splitting the keyboard can also be used to hide it, by tapping on it once.

Don't forget

To unsplit and redock the keyboard, press and hold on the button in Step 1 and tap on the **Dock and Merge** button.

Don't forget

For more information about entering and formatting text with the keyboard, see Chapter Six, pages 116-117.

Multi-Touch Gestures

Since there is no mouse connected to the iPad, navigation is done with the user's fingers. There is a combination of tapping, swiping and pinching gestures that can be used to view items such as web pages, photos, maps and documents and also navigate around the iPad.

Swiping up and down

Swipe up and down with one finger to move up or down web pages, photos, maps or documents. The content moves in the opposite direction of the swipe, i.e. if you swipe up, the page will move down and vice versa.

Tapping and zooming

Double-tap with one finger to zoom in on a web page, photo, map or document. Double-tap again to return to the original view.

Pinching and swiping

Swipe outwards with your thumb and forefinger to zoom in on a
web page, photo, map or document.

Pinch together with your thumb and forefinger to zoom back in.

Pinch together with your thumb
and four fingers to return to the
Home screen from any open app.

Don't forget

Swiping outwards
with your thumb and
forefinger enables you
to zoom in on an item
to a greater degree than
double-tapping with one
finger.

More gestures

- Swipe left or right with four or five fingers to move between open apps

- Swipe up with four or five fingers on the screen to reveal the Multitasking window

- Swipe up from the bottom of the screen to access the Control Center

- Drag with two or three fingers to move a web page, photo, map or document

- Swipe left or right with one finger to move between full-size photos in the Photos app

- Tap once on a photo thumbnail with one finger to enlarge it to full screen within the Photos app

- Drag down at the top-middle of the iPad to view current notifications in the Notification Center

Hot tip

The gestures involving
four or five fingers can
be turned **On** or **Off** in
the **General** section of
the **Settings** app.

iPad Smart Cover

One of the issues with a touchscreen, such as the one on the iPad, is that it is liable to get scratched if it is carried around in a bag or even being moved around in the home. The solution to this is an iPad cover. Being Apple, this not only protects the screen but is designed so that it can also be used as a stand to support the iPad for viewing content or typing with the keyboard.

There is a setting for the iPad cover in the Settings app. This can enable it to lock or unlock the iPad:

1 Tap once on the **Settings** app

Settings

2 Tap once on the **General** tab

General

3 Under **Lock/ Unlock** drag

Lock / Unlock

the button to **On** to enable the cover to lock or unlock the iPad when it is placed in position or removed

Attaching the cover

The iPad cover attaches with a hinge along the left-hand side of the iPad. Attach it by placing the hinge on the side of the iPad until it clicks into place:

Using the cover as a stand

The iPad cover is separated into four foldable panels. These can be folded into a triangular shape to create a stand for the iPad:

Use the stand at the top of the iPad when using the keyboard for input options:

Use the stand at the bottom of the iPad when viewing content such as videos, photos, books or magazines:

Accessories

The iPad is perfectly equipped to be used on its own, without any accessories. However, accessories can not only be fun to add, they can also be functional. Some possible iPad accessories include:

- **Wireless keyboard.** This is an Apple product that is intended primarily for the iMac computer. However, it can be linked to an iPad via Bluetooth and it is a useful option if the iPad is going to be used for a lot of typing, e.g. for essay writing.

48

- **Camera accessories.** If you want to download photos from your own digital camera this can be done with two iPad accessories: a camera connector and a SD card reader. Both of these plug into the slot at the bottom of the iPad where the power cable is attached. The camera connector enables you to download photos and videos directly from a camera while the SD card reader can be used to download content from any SD memory card.

- **iPad Dock.** This is a stand that can be used to position the iPad for viewing content and it can also be used to charge the iPad and connect it to external speakers.

- **Digital AV Adapter (Lightning connector or 30-pin connector).** This can be used to connect your iPad to an HDTV screen so that you can view photos and videos on a large screen. With this adapter the same content on the iPad is played on the TV screen.

- **Apple TV.** This is another way of viewing content from your iPad on your TV. Instead of a cable connection, this is done by streaming video and photos wirelessly to the Apple TV box which then plays it on the TV.

3 iPad Security

Online and physical security are two of a parent's main concerns if their child has an iPad. This chapter details some of the potential dangers and offers advice about combating them. From safer social networking to iPad restrictions, this chapter covers some issues to put your mind at rest.

Areas of Concern

The biggest concern for a parent or teacher of a child with an iPad is that it will be used inappropriately, either by the child themselves or by someone else contacting them via the Web. This falls into two main categories:

- Viewing of inappropriate material

- Contact by strangers on social networking sites, email or messaging sites

Restricting access

Children have always tried to read, look at and watch material that is not necessarily appropriate for their age group. To a degree this is unavoidable but, unfortunately, the Internet has significantly multiplied the amount of inappropriate material that is available. Moreover, a lot of it is significantly beyond the boundaries of what can be considered acceptable.

As shown later in this chapter, there are restrictions that can be put in place to prevent access to certain types of content. But children can be endlessly inventive when it comes to doing things that they shouldn't and nothing is ever completely secure in the world of computing. There may be occasions when they come across inappropriate material, whether it is through online sites with Safari or content in iTunes. Rather than bar these areas completely a good compromise is to put some restrictions in place and discuss with your child what is, and is not, acceptable. You should also have access to the iPad so that you can see what is being viewed: if your child doesn't want to do this it could be an indication that they have something to hide.

Stranger danger

Social networking sites are great for children to keep in touch with their friends, but they can also be a minefield in terms of strangers contacting children, usually under the guise of being their contemporaries. Relationships can then be formed, with the child thinking it is with someone of their own age when the reverse could be true. Also, adults can convince teenage children to meet them or even persuade them to leave home with them.

Dangers on the Internet will never go away but if you are aware of them then you should be able to prevent your child falling prey to some of the malicious practices that are out there.

Beware

It is essential that your child does not form online relationships with people who they do not know, even if the other person claims to be a friend of a friend. If in doubt, your child should be encouraged to tell you about anything with which they are uncomfortable or unsure, no matter how trivial it may seem.

Physical Security

An iPad is a valuable and expensive piece of equipment, particularly for a child to have, so it is important to try to ensure that it is as safe as possible when it is in their possession. This falls into two categories:

- **Safety in the home** – making sure the iPad doesn't get damaged or broken

- **Security outside the home** – making sure the iPad doesn't get lost or stolen

In the home

When your child is using the iPad in the home there are a few rules that should be followed to keep the iPad in good condition:

- **Drinks.** Liquid is the enemy of any piece of electrical equipment so all drinks should be kept well clear of your iPad

- **Hands.** Children have a habit of getting dirty and sticky hands. Make sure that they are always washed, and dried, before your child uses the iPad

- **Cables.** If the iPad is plugged into anything (for charging or transferring files) make sure that the cables are away from feet and legs, so that they do not get caught up

Away from home

There will be many occasions when your child will want to take the iPad away from home, either to use with their friends or to take to school. Some issues to consider about this:

- **Plain bag.** Keep it as inconspicuous as possible and carry it in a plain bag so that it is out of sight

- **Know the serial number.** If the iPad is lost or stolen make sure you know the serial number so that you can quote this if it is found. This is located within the **General > About** section of the Settings app, under **Serial Number**

- **Keep it with you.** Stress to your child the importance of keeping the iPad with them. Do not give it to other people or leave it unattended in a bag

- **Report any loss.** If the iPad is lost or stolen, ensure that your child tells you as soon as possible so you can take any action

A lot of companies offer specific insurance for iPads and you should also check to see if it is covered by your home and contents insurance.

Finding Your iPad

If the worst comes to the worst and your iPad is lost or stolen, help is at hand. The Find My iPad function (operated through the online iCloud service) allows you to send a sound alert to a lost iPad and also remotely lock it or even wipe its contents. This gives added peace of mind, knowing that even if your iPad is lost or stolen its contents will not necessarily be compromised.
To set up Find My iPad:

Don't forget

To use the Find My iPad service you need to have an iCloud account. This is free and can be obtained by accessing the **Account** section under the iCloud link in Step 2. You also need an Apple ID to set up an iCloud account.

52

Hot tip

A similar service to Find My iPad comes from the Lookout app. This can be downloaded from the App Store and once you have registered you can send an alert to your iPad by going to the Lookout website at www.mylookout.com

① Tap once on the **Settings** app

② Tap once on the **iCloud** link

③ Drag this button to **On** to be able to find your iPad on a map and send messages to it remotely

Find My iPad

④ Tap once on the **OK** button to enable the Find My iPad functionality

> **Find My iPad**
> This enables Find My iPad features, including the ability to show the location of this iPad on a map.
>
> | Cancel | OK |

Finding a lost iPad

Once you have set up Find My iPad you can search for it through the online iCloud service. To do this:

① Log in to your iCloud account at **www.icloud.com**

② Tap once on the **Find My iPhone** button (this also works for the iPad)

3 Tap once on the **All Devices** button and select your iPad. It is identified and its current location is displayed on the map

4 Tap once on the green circle to view details about when your iPad was located

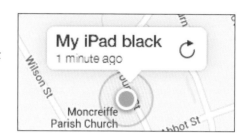

5 Tap once here to send a sound alert to your iPad

Hot tip

Tap once on the **Erase iPad** button in Step 5 to delete the contents of your iPad so that no-one else can access them.

53

6 Tap once here to lock your iPad remotely

7 Enter a passcode so that no-one else can access the contents on your iPad

Locking Your iPad

If you are worried about your iPad falling into the wrong hands, and its information being compromised, it is possible to set a passcode so that no-one can access the contents of the iPad without the correct code. To do this:

Hot tip

If you set a passcode for locking and unlocking your iPad, agree it with your child so you both know. Otherwise you will have to unlock the iPad every time your child wants to use it, or they will be able to lock it so that you cannot access it.

1 Tap once on the **Settings** app

2 Tap once on the **General** link

3 Tap once on the **Passcode Lock** button

Passcode Lock	Off >

4 Tap once on the **Turn Passcode On** link

5 Enter the passcode and re-enter it to confirm it

Don't forget

Once the passcode has been set, tap once on the **Require Passcode** button to specify when the passcode is activated. This can be immediately, or over a period of minutes or hours.

6 The passcode has to be entered to access the iPad for use every time it has been locked

Viruses

As far as security from viruses on the iPad is concerned there is good news and bad news:

- The good news is that, due to its architecture, most apps on the iPad do not communicate with each other so, even if there were a virus, it is unlikely that it would infect the whole iPad. Also, there are relatively few viruses being aimed at the iPad, particularly compared with those for Windows PCs.

- The bad news is that no computer system is immune from viruses and malware and complacency is one of the biggest enemies of computer security. Also, as iPads become more popular, and more widely used, they become a more attractive target for hackers and virus writers.

Malware is short for malicious software, which is designed to harm your computer or gain access to information on it.

iPad security

Apple takes security on the iPad very seriously and one way that this manifests itself is in the fact it is designed so that different apps do not talk to each other. This means that if there was a virus in an app then it would be hard for it to transfer to others and therefore spread across the iPad. Apple's own apps are the exception to this, but as they are developed and checked by Apple there is very little chance of them being infected by viruses.

Apple also checks apps that are provided through the App Store and this process is very robust. This does not mean that it is impossible for a virus to infect the iPad (but there have not been any so far) so keep an eye on the Apple website to see if there are any details about iPad viruses.

Antivirus options

There are few apps in the App Store that deal with antivirus issues, although not actually removing viruses, due to the lack of iPad viruses in circulation. Some options to look at:

- **VirusBarrier.** This checks files that are copied onto your iPad, via email or online services, to ensure that they are virus-free

- **McAfee Global Threat Intelligence Mobile.** This is not technically an antivirus app, but it does provide a daily update about new viruses that are in circulation

- **Anti-Virus Detective.** This is an app that has a step-by-step process to identify suspected viruses or malware

Online Security

Organizations for online security

The issue of online security for children is taken extremely seriously by governments and police forces around the world. There are police taskforces to monitor exploitation on the Internet and organizations that offer advice and help.

One site that offers a range of advice about safety on the Web is the Child Exploitation and Online Protection Centre. Their website can be found at **ceop.police.uk**:

Don't forget

Different countries will have their own websites dedicated to child safety on the Internet. Type **Internet Child Safety** into an Internet search engine to find appropriate sites in your own location.

Tap once on this icon to access the CEOP Internet Safety Centre

This has advice for all age groups and also a link to report problems directly to CEOP:

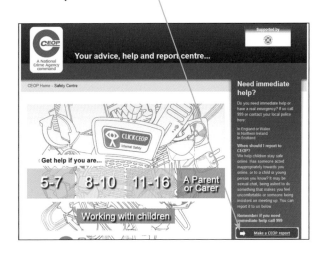

56

CEOP also has its own age-specific websites (Thinkuknow) covering web safety, while still being able to get the most out of your web experience. Each of the age-specific sites can be accessed from the CEOP Homepage.

Don't forget

CEOP has a list of links to other useful sites concerned with online child safety on the Web.

Some of the key issues dealt with by sites like CEOP are:

- Know how your child is accessing online content and, if possible, have them do this somewhere in the home where you are, so that it is not a secret.

- Talk to your child about the issues to do with online safety and also how they use the Web. Create a partnership in terms of web use and generate an atmosphere of trust with your child so that they can feel confident and secure when accessing content on the Web. Using the Web should be fun and this involves both you and your child feeling secure and confident about their online activities.

- Encourage your child to tell you anything with which they are unhappy or unsure. Reassure them that they will not get into trouble for doing this and that it is never wrong to flag up something they are concerned about.

- Know how to report your own concerns. Either do this directly on a website, or to your child's school, through CEOP or, ultimately, to the police. No matter how trivial you think something may seem, it is always worth reporting it if it makes you uneasy or you think there is the possibility that someone is acting inappropriately towards a child online.

Social Networking Safety

Safety on social networking sites, particularly with the range of sites now available (see Chapter Nine, pages 198-200), can be a major concern for parents and teachers. Talk to your child about this as much as possible and be open with each other about your concerns and views. Some of the main issues to consider are:

- Some sites have a minimum age limit for joining. However, there is no way for the site to enforce this and so the only realistic way is through parental control. Despite this it would still be possible for children under the age limit to open an account at their friends' houses or other locations. So, in some ways, if a younger child is asking for an account on a site with a minimum age it is sometimes better to allow this so that you can have some control over what they are doing.

- If you have your own account on social networking sites it is perfectly possible to be included as one of your child's contacts so that you can view their pages (known as friends on some sites). They may have their own views on this but it can be a good compromise for younger children particularly. However, your child may still be able to communicate with their peers via private messaging.

- Never communicate with someone you don't know. People can set up fake accounts, so if you are contacted by someone you don't know, then ignore it.

- Never advertise parties or social gatherings at your home through social media. A lot of small social gatherings have been escalated into chaotic parties in this way.

- Things that are on social networking sites can stay there permanently if they are not removed. Some employers now search the social networking sites of prospective employees to see if there is anything untoward there. This can go back several years.

- Nothing is private. Photos and comments can be copied and distributed to people via other means, such as email. Even private messages can be copied.

- Even if you are annoyed with someone, don't post inappropriate comments about them. This can quickly get out of control and cause a lot of problems for all concerned.

Beware

Cyberbullying is one of the main concerns on the Web and particularly on social networking sites. Encourage your child to tell you about anything that is upsetting or worrying them. However, children can also be bullied, and feel excluded, if they are not part of the social networking community.

Beware

Always make sure that you log out of any social networking account whenever you are away from your iPad. If not, someone could access your account and post messages, or photos, pretending to be you. On Facebook, this is known as a 'frape', which is a contraction of 'Facebook rape'. Even if this is done in a humorous way, it can cause huge problems.

Safer Browsing

The default browser for web content on the iPad is Safari. However, the Mobicip Safe Browser can be downloaded from the App Store to ensure safer browsing for children. To do this:

1 Download the Mobicip app and tap once on this button

2 When you first access the app you have to register with Mobicip. At this point you can also apply settings for your child. You can also do this by accessing the Mobicip website at **www.mobicip.com**
Tap once on the Add Another User button

3 Enter the name of your child and tap here to specify their school level

4 Once in the Mobicip browser, tap once here and tap on the **Settings** link

5 Tap once on a child's name to enable them to use the browser. You have to log in to your account each time you want to change a user

6 If inappropriate content is attempted to be accessed, this message appears

Hot tip

Within the Mobicip browser, tap once on this button on the bottom toolbar to access the Mobicip Homepage, where there are links to child-friendly websites.

Restrictions

Within the iPad Settings there are a number of options for restricting types of content that can be viewed and also actions that can be performed. These include:

- Turning off certain apps so that they cannot be used

- Enabling changes to certain functions

- Restricting content that is viewed using specific apps

When setting restrictions, they can be locked so that children cannot change them back or set them themselves. To do this:

Hot tip

If you put restrictions in place on the iPad it is a good idea to talk to your child about it and explain what you are doing and why. If you are honest and open with them then hopefully they will be the same with you.

60

1 Tap once on the **Settings** app

2 Tap once on the **General** link

3 Tap once on the **Restrictions** link

4 The restrictions are grayed-out, i.e. they have not been enabled for use yet

5 Tap once on the **Enable Restrictions** link

6 Type on the keypad to set a passcode for enabling and disabling Restrictions

7 Re-enter the passcode

Beware

If you forget the passcode for unlocking your iPad it will become disabled for a period of time after you have entered the wrong passcode a number of times. Eventually, it will lock completely.
It can be reset by using a computer with which the iPad was last synced and there are details about this on the Apple website Support pages. However, to avoid this, ensure that you have a note of the iPad's passcode, but keep it away from the iPad.

8 All of the Restrictions options become available

Allowing Apps

One of the biggest security concerns for parents or teachers of children using an iPad is that they will use certain apps to access inappropriate content or use them for activities such as messaging or video chatting with strangers. If you are concerned about this, certain apps can be turned off so that they cannot be used at all. To do this:

1 Access the Restrictions section as shown on the previous two pages

2 Drag these buttons to turn a specific app **On** or **Off**

Don't forget

If the buttons within the **Settings** app are green, this mean that the selected item is **On**.

3 When an app is turned off it is removed entirely from the Home screen

Don't forget

If an app is turned off, it retains any settings that have been applied to it, e.g. bookmarks in Safari will still be there if you turn the app back on.

4 This option also enables you to turn **On** or **Off** the ability

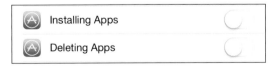

to install and delete apps. If these are turned **Off** then no new apps can be installed from the App Store, or deleted from the iPad

Allowing Changes

These restrictions enable you to turn on or off whether the iPad's location can be used for certain functions and whether changes can be made to Mail, Contacts and the Calendar apps. Generally, the location option gives more functionality to certain apps, such as maps, and it is generally a useful thing to have turned on. To enable these changes:

1 Access the **Restrictions** section

2 Select an option under **Privacy** to allow changes for specific apps. Select **Accounts** under **Allow Changes** to allow changes in **Mail, Contacts and Calendars**

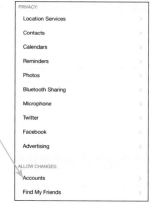

3 For each item tap once on the **Allow Changes** link

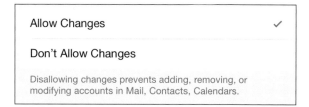

4 For **Location Services**, drag this button to **On** to enable Wi-Fi hotspots to identify the location of the iPad when you are using it in a different location

Don't forget

For Location Services, each app that depends on a location is listed and can be turned on or off accordingly.

Allowing Content

Another parental concern about children using an iPad is about striking the right balance between letting them get as much benefit out of it, while ensuring that they do not view inappropriate content. One way to do this is to restrict the type of content that is available to view. This is done by selecting an appropriate ratings system for your location and then specifying the type of content that can be viewed for music, movies, TV shows and apps. To do this:

Don't forget

You should select the country in which you are located, but experimenting with other countries is a good way to see the types of movie and TV ratings they have.

1 Access the **Restrictions** section

2 Under **Allowed Content**, tap once on the **Ratings For** link

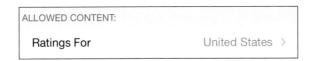

ALLOWED CONTENT:

Ratings For   United States >

3 Tap once on the country for which you want the ratings to apply

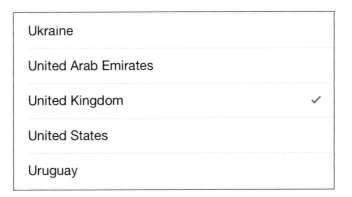

Ukraine

United Arab Emirates

United Kingdom   ✓

United States

Uruguay

4 Tap once on the **Restrictions** button to go back (this should be done after each restriction item has been selected)

< Restrictions

5 Tap once on the **Music, Podcasts & iTunes U** link

| Music, Podcasts & iTunes U | Explicit > |

6 Drag this button to **Off** to block any music or podcasts from the iTunes Store with explicit content

MUSIC, PODCASTS & ITUNES U MEDIA RATED:

EXPLICIT

Allow Playback of Music, Music Videos, Podcasts and iTunes U media containing Explicit Content.

7 Tap once on the **Movies** link

| Movies | All > |

8 The movie ratings system for the country selected in Step 3 is displayed. Tap once on the rating up to which you want content to be displayed. The ones after it will then be blocked

ALLOW MOVIES RATED:

Don't Allow Movies	
U	✓
PG	✓
12	✓
15	
18	
Allow All Movies	

Don't forget

Music and podcasts with explicit content are marked appropriately within the iTunes Store. However, if this is turned off within Restrictions Settings, these items cannot be played even when previewed in the iTunes Store.

65

...cont'd

9 Tap once on the **TV Shows** link

TV Shows	All >

10 Tap once on the rating up to which you want content to be displayed

ALLOW TV SHOWS RATED:

Don't Allow TV Shows

CAUTION ✓

Allow All TV Shows

Don't forget

In-App purchases consist of apps that contain additional content that has to be purchased. For instance, you may download a free painting app that has some free samples to use to paint over. There may then be additional samples that have to be purchased. Games, magazines and books frequently have in-app purchases.

11 Drag this button to **Off** to block any In-App Purchases

In-App Purchases

12 If In-App Purchases are turned On, tap once on the **Require Password** link and set an option for when a password has to be entered if buying In-App Purchases

Require Password	15 minutes >
Require password for purchases.	

4 Apps and the App Store

Apps are the lifeblood of the iPad and enable you to do everything on it, from work to play and everything in between. This chapter shows how to use iPad apps and download new ones.

Introducing the App Store

While the built-in apps that come with the iPad are flexible and versatile, it really comes into its own when you connect to the App Store. This is an online resource and there are thousands of apps here that can be downloaded and then used on your iPad, including a wealth of both education and entertainment apps.

To use the App Store, you must first have an Apple ID. This can be obtained when you first connect to the App Store. Once you have an Apple ID you can start exploring the App Store.

Don't forget

For details on how to obtain an Apple ID see page 21.

1 Tap once on this icon on the Home screen

2 The latest available apps are displayed on the Homepage of the App Store, including featured and Editors' Choice apps

Beware

The content in the iPad App Store is not identical to that available from Apple computers, the iMac and MacBooks. While some of the apps are the same, they are developed specifically for the different systems.

3 Tap on these buttons to view the apps according to these headings

4 Tap on these buttons to view items according to these categories

Viewing Apps

Once you have accessed the App Store you can then start
exploring the apps that are available:

1 Tap once on an app

2 General details about the
app are displayed

3 Swipe left or right
here to view additional
information about the app
and view details from it

4 Reviews
and
related
apps are
available
at the
top of
the page

By default, the App Store
opens on the Featured
items page.

For more information
about finding apps, see
pages 72-74.

Downloading Apps

When you identify an app that you, or your child, would like to use it can be downloaded to your iPad. To do this:

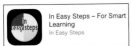
1 Find the app you want to download and tap once on this button (this will say Free or have a price)

2 The button changes to say **Install**. Tap on this once

3 Enter your Apple ID details and tap once on the **OK** button (apps cannot be downloaded without this, so your child cannot download their own apps)

4 The app will begin to download on your iPad

5 Once the app is downloaded tap once on it to open and use it

Categories of Apps

Within the App Store, apps are separated into categories according to type. This enables you to find apps according to particular subjects. To do this:

1 Tap once on the **More** button on the toolbar at the top of the App Store

2 The categories are listed alphabetically

New apps are added to all categories on a regular basis, so keep checking back to see what is new.

3 Tap once on a category to see the apps within it

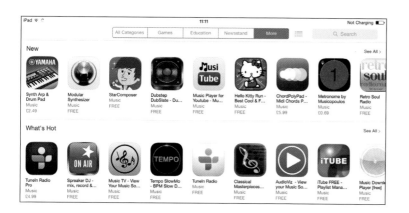

Finding Apps

As well as looking through apps in specific categories you can also find them in other ways too.

Top Charts

To find the top paid for and free apps:

Don't forget

Some apps will differ depending on the geographical location from where you are accessing the App Store.

1 Tap once on the **Top Charts** button on the toolbar at the bottom of the App Store

2 The top overall paid for and free apps are displayed

3 To find the top apps in different categories, tap once on this button

4 Tap once on a category

5 The top apps for that category are displayed

Near Me

This is a feature which suggests appropriate apps according to your current geographic location. To use this:

1 Tap once on the **Near Me** button on the toolbar at the bottom of the App Store

2 Tap once on the **Show Popular Apps Near Me** link

3 Tap once on the **OK** button to enable the App Store to use your location (**Location Services** has to be turned **On**)

4 Recommendations will appear in the **Popular Near Me** window, based on your location

Depending on your location, there may not be any apps featured in the **Near Me** section.

...cont'd

Searching for apps

Another way to find apps is with the App Store Search box, which is located at the top-right corner of the App Store window. To use this:

Hot tip

When searching for apps, the results are displayed with an **iPad Only** button or an **iPhone Only** button at the top of the window. Tap on the **iPhone Only** button if you do not see what you are looking for under iPad apps. These apps can also be used on an iPad.

1 Tap once in the **Search** box to bring up the iPad keyboard

2 Enter a search keyword or phrase

3 Suggested apps appear as you are typing. Tap once on an app to view it

Sorting

Within search results it is possible to sort the apps according to specific criteria. To do this:

Don't forget

By default, apps are sorted by **Relevance**.

1 Select an item from the search results as above

2 Tap once on these buttons to sort the suggested apps according to these criteria

3 Tap once on one of the buttons to view the sort options

Organizing Apps

When you start downloading apps you will probably soon find that you have dozens, if not hundreds, of them. You can move between screens to view all of your apps by swiping left or right with one finger.

Hot tip

To move an app between screens, tap and hold on it until it starts to jiggle and a cross appears in the corner. Then drag it to the side of the screen. If there is space on the next screen then the app will be moved there.

As more apps are added it can become hard to find the apps you want, particularly if you have to swipe between several screens. However, it is possible to organize apps into individual folders to make using them more manageable. To do this:

1 Press on an app until it starts to jiggle and a white cross appears at the top-left corner

2 Drag the app over another one

Don't forget

As in real life, children can sometimes prefer downloading apps rather than organizing them. So, from time to time, you may need to create some new folders to keep the Home screen tidy. Think of it as tidying a virtual bedroom!

...cont'd

3 A folder is created, containing the two apps

4 The folder is given a default name, usually based on the category of the apps

5 Tap on the folder name and type a new name if required

6 Click the **Home button** once to finish creating the folder

7 Click the **Home button** again to return to the Home screen (this is done whenever you want to return to the Home screen from an apps folder)

8 The folder is added on the Home screen. Tap on this once to access the items within it

76

Updating Apps

The world of apps is a dynamic and fast-moving one and new apps are being created and added to the App Store on a daily basis. Existing apps are also being updated, to improve their performance and functionality. Once you have installed an app from the App Store, updates can be downloaded free of charge. To do this:

1 When an update is available it is denoted by the red icon on the App Store button, showing how many updates are available

2 Tap once on the **App Store** button

3 In the App Store, tap once on the **Updates** button

4 The available updates are displayed

5 Tap once on the **Update** button to update an app

6 Tap once on the **Update All** button to update all of the required apps

Update All

Don't forget

When updates are available the red icon on the App Store button will appear automatically so that you will always know when there are new updates, unless you have turned on **Automatic Downloads**, see below.

77

Hot tip

It is possible to set updates to apps to be downloaded automatically: **Settings > iTunes & App Stores > Automatic Downloads**. Drag the button to **On** for the required items.

Deleting Apps

If you decide that you do not want certain apps anymore, they can be deleted from your iPad. However, they remain in the iCloud so that you can reinstall them if you change your mind. This also means that if you delete an app by mistake you can get it back from the App Store without having to pay for it again. To do this:

Beware

If you delete an app it will also delete any data that has been compiled with that app, even if you reinstall it from the App Store.

1 Press on an app until it starts to jiggle and a white cross appears at the top-left corner

2 Tap once on this cross to delete the app. In the Delete dialog box, tap once on the **Delete** button

Delete "Pages"

Deleting "Pages" will also delete all of its data from this iPad. Any documents & data stored in iCloud will not be deleted and can be managed in Settings.

Delete   Cancel

3 Tap once on the **App Store** button

Don't forget

You cannot delete any of the in-built iPad apps.

4 Tap once on the **Purchased** button

Purchased

5 Apps that have been deleted have this iCloud icon next to them

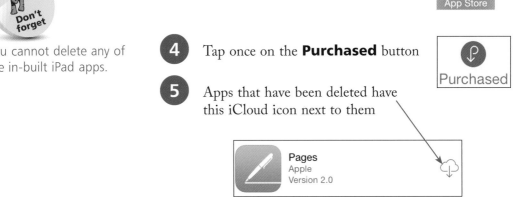

Pages
Apple
Version 2.0

6 Tap once on the **iCloud** button to reinstall an app

5 Educational Apps

The world of education is usually enthusiastic about embracing new technology and this is certainly true of the iPad. There is now a whole range of educational apps for all ages. This chapter shows the types of apps that can be used by both pre-school and high school children.

Using Educational Apps

For many adults, who have grown up thinking that all education involves using a pen and paper, the idea of using a gadget such as an iPad for educational purposes may seem a little frivolous. But times change and not only are children beginning to use mobile devices for all aspects of their lives, education establishments are now starting to use iPads and apps in mainstream education. As a parent, it is a revolution that cannot be avoided so it is best to embrace it with open arms and try to help your child get the most out of the iPad for educational purposes.

The rules have changed

Due to the multimedia nature of the iPad, the way in which it can be used for education is different from more traditional methods of classroom learning. For the older generation, education was usually done in two separate ways:

- Books, paper and pens for learning
- Toys for learning through play

With apps on the iPad these two methods are usually combined so you have a mixture of traditional learning methods, incorporated with games, puzzles and quizzes. Add in photos, videos and animations and it is easy to see why the iPad can be such an attractive learning tool for children.

Try out the lite version

Since there are thousands of educational apps available it can sometimes be overwhelming trying to find the best ones for your child. One option for this is to try the lite version of an app. This is a free version of a paid-for app. The lite version only has some of the functionality of the full app but it will give you a flavor of it so that you can have a good idea about whether you want to buy the paid-for version or not. Lite versions of apps are usually identified with the word Lite on their icons within the App Store:

Hot tip

The App Store has Quick Links at the bottom of the Featured page for **Kids** apps, covering different age groups.

Working with Your Child

It is important that you are involved with any learning activities that your child is doing on the iPad. Obviously, this does not mean that you have to do everything with them, all of the time, and the age of your child will determine to some extent the amount of parental input. For younger children you will probably want to go through the learning process with them, while as they get older yours may become a more advisory role. Some of the ways that parents, grandparents or teachers can be involved are:

- **Helping to find the best educational apps.** You can do some research into this on your own but ultimately the best option is to find them with your child too.

- **Providing help and guidance where required.** You should be up to speed on what each educational app offers so that you can help use the app and also discuss the subject matter.

- **Reviewing work and learning outcomes that have been undertaken.** A lot of apps have tests and quizzes so you can see how your child is dealing with the subject.

- **Knowing when to step back and let your child get on with things on their own.** In any learning environment there is a fine line between providing assistance and being overbearing. Try to be there when needed but allow your child their own space to explore different apps at their own pace.

Getting the right apps

When choosing educational apps, there may be some initial disagreement between you and your child: you may want the ones that look like they have the most educational benefit, while your child may gravitate towards the ones that look the most fun. Thankfully, with the majority of the iPad educational apps, the learning and the fun elements are combined so it should be easier to reach a consensus about the best apps to use. Since your child is the one who is going to be using the app the most, it is only reasonable to let them have their own input into obtaining apps. There may be times when you will have to compromise and go with their choice.

It is also a good idea to talk to your child's teacher when choosing apps. They may have some ideas of their own and they will be able to make suggestions based on what is being taught at that time.

Don't forget

The majority of educational apps are generally inexpensive so you should not spend a fortune even if you use several of them.

Following School Curricula

One area of great interest to parents and teachers will be the ways in which an iPad can be used to complement the work done for the school curriculum, particularly with a view to sitting exams.

Depending on your geographic location, there may be a range of apps that are specific to your country's education system. Some of these may be linked into existing websites that offer resources for your education system.

Finding relevant material

Hot tip

Always speak to your child's teachers to see which apps they recommend in terms of following the subjects that are currently being taught. They may also have suggestions for websites that are linked into the learning activities. These websites are frequently linked into the apps for the iPad.

If you search for apps based on your country's education system you will be able to see any apps that are available for this. For instance, apps for the K–12 system, which is used in the USA, Canada and most parts of Australia, can be found by entering this as a search keyword:

Apps can cover the whole education system in general or you could search for specific years, such as K–5:

82

For the UK, enter keywords relevant to the exams that are taken, i.e. GCSEs, A Levels, Standard Grades or Highers

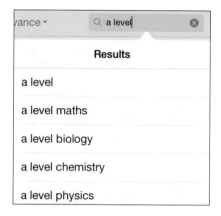

For A Level students there is a range of apps that are linked to the Examstutor website. This is an online learning resource that can be found at **www.examstutor.com**

Some apps for A Level subjects have to be accessed from the iPhone Apps button in the App Store. However, they can also be used on the iPad.

The apps mirror the content on the main website and require the login details that the students use when they log in to the main site

About Pre-School Apps

For children under school age there is a range of educational apps designed to start teaching them the basics of reading, writing and arithmetic. There are also apps for skills such as drawing and painting.

Pre-school apps are located in the main Education category in the App Store and can be found in a variety of ways:

1 Enter appropriate keywords into the Search box

2 Relevant suggestions are made based on the keywords. Tap on one of the suggestions to view that app

or

1 Tap once on the **Top Charts** button at the bottom of the App Store window

2 Tap once on the **All Categories** button and select **Education**. Within the top apps, there are some apps that are appropriate for pre-school or kindergarten children

Don't forget

Icons for pre-school apps are usually in the form of cartoon art so they are easy to recognize when being viewed alongside other apps.

Assessing apps

Once you have found an app in which you are interested:

1 Tap on it once

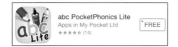

2 Read the description
and view the details
to assess whether
you think it will be
appropriate

If an app is free
it is always worth
downloading it so
that you can assess its
effectiveness. If you do
not like it you can always
then delete it.

Some pre-school apps also have parental guides, or a parent zone,
that can be ordered once you have downloaded the app itself.
These offer advice about using the app with your child and how to
get the most out of the learning experience with them.

Pre-School Apps

The following is a selection of pre-school apps covering reading, writing, counting and learning games. There are hundreds of other similar apps – the ones here indicate the range that is available and also the type of functionality they provide.

PocketPhonics
This is an app for learning to write. To use it:

Don't forget

Pre-school apps usually have buttons to take you back to the Homepage, or a main menu, such as this one:

1 Tap once on this icon

pocketp...cslite

2 Tap once on the **Play** button

3 Tap once on a letter

4 The letter is displayed and the app shows how to write it. Audio narration accompanies this

Say then watch how to write.

5 Drag over the letter with a finger to write it yourself on the iPad

Write with your finger.

TapToTalk

This is an app for learning to talk. To use it:

1   Tap once on this icon

2   Tap once on one of the categories

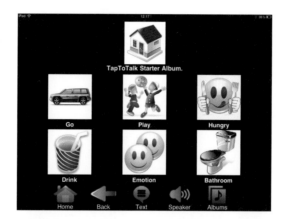

3   Tap once on an item. The phrase appears at the top and is spoken by the app. The audio can be turned off so that your child can say the phrase for themselves

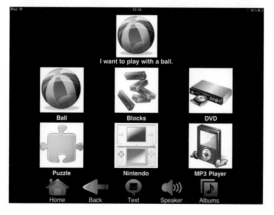

4   Tap on these buttons to go to the Homepage, go back one page, turn off text or audio and go to the albums section

...cont'd

AB Math

This is an app for learning basic arithmetic. To use it:

1 Tap once on this icon

2 Select an option for the type of sums that you want to do

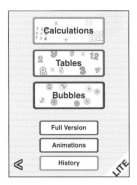

A lot of mathematics apps have games and scores to make the learning activities more fun. This is a good way to judge your child's progress with the app.

3 Select a level of difficulty and tap on the **Play** button

4 Enter an answer for the sums that appear. A green tick appears if the answer is correct and the next sum appears automatically

ABC SpellingMagic

This is an app for learning to spell. To use it:

 Tap once on this icon

SpellingMagic

2 Select settings for the app and tap once on this arrow to start the app

3 Tap once on a letter item

4 An item and its letters are displayed, including boxes for the letters

5 Drag the letters into the boxes to create the word. Tap once on the arrow to move to the next word

...cont'd

Pre-School Classroom

This is an app for learning a range of skills, including reading, writing, arithmetic and matching items. To use it:

1 Tap once on this icon

2 Tap once on this button (or the **Play** button)

3 Enter the name of the person who will be using the app and tap once on the **Play** button

4 Follow the instructions for games such as matching objects with each other by drawing lines between them

5 For word games, tap once on a letter to match each object correctly

Read Me Stories

This is a reading app that provides stories that can either be read by your child or automatically by the app. To use it:

1   Tap once on this icon

2   Tap once on a book to go to that series

3   Tap once on a book within a series

Narrated stories can be a good learning tool and an excellent way to keep your child occupied. However, some of the voices used for the narration can become annoying after a while.

4   Tap once on one of the buttons to select whether you want your child to listen to the book being read, or read it for themselves

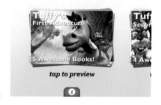

5   If the book is being read by the app, the words are highlighted as it is being read so that it can be followed by your child

Mathematics Apps

There are numerous mathematics apps that are not only very educational, but also a lot of fun!

MathBoard

This is one of the top mathematics apps and it can be used through a range of ages. It generates sets of quizzes, with the difficulty of the questions based on settings that are specified by the user. To use it:

Don't forget

There are also a lot of apps for practising times tables. These contain times tables questions with multiple choice answers, or options for the user to add their own answers.

92

1 Tap once on this icon

MathBoard

2 Settings are positioned on the left-hand side

Settings
OPERATOR TYPES
(+ -)
PROBLEMS
(25, Vertical, Multiple Choice)
NUMBER RANGE
(1-50)
DIGIT LIMIT
Off
TIME
(Elapsed)
EXTRAS
Math Tables & Problem Solver
MORE FROM PALASOFTWARE
Student

Hot tip

The default multiple choice answer option can be changed in the **Settings > Problems**. Options can be selected under **Answer Style**.

3 Tap once on the **Play** button to start a quiz

< Play >

4 By default, the questions have multiple choice answers. Tap once on a answer. The results so far for the quiz are shown to the left of the current question

Results
1) 45 - 41 = 4
2) 49 - 1 = 48
3) 33 - 12 = 21
4) 33 + 2 = 35
5) 29 + 41 = 70
6) 47 + 31 = ___

47
+ 31

a. 68
b. 84
c. 76
d. 82
e. 78

5 To the left of the questions and results is a chalkboard. This can be used to work out the current sum. Write with your finger on the chalkboard to create the sum

6 Tap once on a setting to select different options. The more options that are selected then the harder the questions in the quizzes. For instance, if more Operator Types are checked on then this will increase the types of questions that are included in the quiz

Don't forget

Student names can be added at the bottom of the Settings sections, so that different people can have their own accounts and results.

7 Tap once on the **Extras** Setting to access Tables and also the Problem Solver. This can be used to add specific sums and view the working for solving them

8 Tables, such as the multiplication table, can be used for general reference and revision

...cont'd

Beware

If the Problem Solver is used while you are in the middle of a quiz, that question will be marked as incorrect.

9 The sums become harder when more options are selected within the Settings

10 If a sum is too complicated, tap once on the **Show Problem** link at the bottom left-hand corner

11 The Problem Solver shows the full working for a specific sum. This is an excellent way to find out the technique for working out types of sums

Math Bingo

This is a bingo-based game that tests adding, subtraction, multiplication and division. To use it:

1 Tap once on this icon

2 Tap once on the **Play** button

3 Tap once on an existing player or tap once on the Player button and add details for a new player

4 Select the type of game you want to play. Tap once on the yellow box to use a combination

5 Select a skill level

6 The questions appear at the top of the board. Tap once on an answer. When you have completed a column or a row, the word BINGO appears across it

Math Bingo is a fun way of introducing younger children to more complex sums, particularly with the different skill levels.

English Apps

There are a lot of apps related to studying English as a subject, as opposed to as a foreign language. These generally fall into three categories:

- **Apps for specific exam syllabus**, i.e. relevant to certain countries or examination boards

- **Course study notes or companions**, i.e. apps that help with set texts, such as Shakespeare and John Steinbeck

- **Reference material**, such as dictionaries and grammar guides

Apps for English exams

To find apps for specific exam boards:

1 Enter the name of the exam board in the **App Store Search box** to find relevant apps

2 Apps for the relevant syllabus can be reviewed and downloaded if required

...cont'd

Course notes

To find course study notes for relevant English texts:

1 Enter the name of the text in the **App Store Search box** to find relevant apps

2 Course study notes for the relevant text can be reviewed and downloaded if required

Reference material

This can be found under the Reference category in the App Store:

1 Search for the type of reference material you want to use

2 Reference items can be reviewed and downloaded if required

Don't forget

A lot of good dictionaries can be found in the **Reference** category. Some of the better ones usually require a fee.

Science Apps

Apps for biology, chemistry and physics generally take the form of lessons and tests in the relevant subjects, at different levels.

Finding science apps

To search for science apps, enter the name of the discipline, or a branch of it, into the App Store Search box. Relevant apps are displayed and can then be reviewed:

Don't forget

Some science apps have lessons in the form of multiple choice questions, with descriptions and explanations after each question has been answered.

Style of science apps

Generally, science apps are in the form of interactive lessons:

1 Tap once on an item to open it within the app

2 Select a topic and tap once on the **Begin** (or **Start**) button to begin the lesson

3 The lesson is displayed, either with textual explanations, or a narration, or both

4 The lesson proceeds automatically (like a video that can be paused as you are progressing) until the topic has been completed. (In some apps the lesson may have to be advanced manually with a **Next** button to move to the next item.)

Some science apps have tests that can be done at the end of each section.

Science reference apps

There are several general reference apps, with one of the most useful being the periodic table of elements. Tap once on one of the elements to see its properties:

History Apps

History apps generally fall into two categories:

- This day in history apps

- Topic apps, covering specific areas of history or topics

This day in history

These are apps that contain information for what happened on a certain day in history. This includes notable events, discoveries, wars and birthdays of famous people:

This day in history apps are very useful for finding out specific facts. However, they do not provide any critical analysis of events, which might be required for following a history syllabus at school.

Topic apps

To find apps for specific history topics:

1 Enter the name of a historical topic in the **App Store Search box** to find relevant apps

2 The app contains main topic headings for each subject

3 Within a history topic app, tap once on one of the main topic headings

Beware

Apps that have a lot of text, such as those for history lessons, do not always have a Print function. If you want to print out the text then it has to be copied to an app that can do this, such as Pages. For details about how to do this, see Chapter Six.

4 Information about the selected topic is displayed. Swipe up and down with one finger to move through the topic

Geography Apps

Apps for geography students generally fall into two categories:

- General geography

- Topic apps. These are apps that cover specific areas of geography such as geology or environmental geography

In addition to this, there is also a geography app that is possibly the best educational game for the iPad – Stack the Countries (see page 104).

One of the best overall geography apps is the Geography Encyclopedia. To use this:

1 Tap once on this icon

2 Tap once on the main screen to move to the categories section

3 Main topic headings are shown on the top menu bar, with the categories for each below them. Tap once on a category to go to that topic

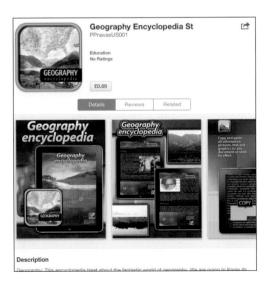

4 Information about the selected topic is displayed. Swipe up and down with one finger to move through the topic

103

Hot tip

As with web pages, content within the Geography Encyclopedia app can be zoomed in on by double-tapping with one finger.

5 Each topic has text, diagrams and photos to illustrate different points and areas

...cont'd

Stack the Countries

This is an educational game that combines multiple choice geography questions and elements of one of the best computer games of all time, Tetris. It is dangerously addictive, for children and adults alike! To use it:

Don't forget

Tetris is a simple but addictive computer game involving falling shapes that are fitted together to create lines. There is an iPad version.

Beware

When a country icon is dropped it bounces on the stand at the bottom. Depending on the shape of the icon, and the position in which it is dropped, it can bounce off the stand completely.

1 Tap once on this icon

2 Multiple choice questions appear at the top of the screen. Tap once on an icon to select an answer

3 If the answer is correct, the country icon is selected. Drag on it to rotate or move its position

4 Tap once on the **Drop It!** button to drop the country icon onto the stand at the bottom. Build up the country icons until they reach the dotted line, at which point the game is completed and you gain a new country to study

Language Apps

Apps for learning foreign languages generally fall into two categories:

- Study apps

- Flashcards, principally for learning vocabulary

Study apps

These are apps that cover a comprehensive learning solution for foreign languages, including:

- Online tutorials

- Study notes

- Audio repetition

- Flashcards

- Text quizzes

- Audio quizzes

Full study apps for learning a foreign language are usually paid for apps, while flashcards are more likely to be free.

Flashcards

These are apps that deliver vocabulary details for the selected language. They can either be in the form of text cards, similar to a dictionary, or they can be audio cards where the selected words have an audio accompaniment.

Some More to Try

There are literally thousands of apps in each category of the App Store. The ones below are just a small range of some more education apps for children of different ages.

- **Color Uncovered.** An app that contains some fascinating information about color, how it works and how we interact with it. The topics contain an image with a question and then a textual explanation.

Hot tip

When searching for apps, sometimes two words are run together to create the name of the app, e.g. GoSkyWatch.

- **Dragon Dictation.** This is a useful app for any children who have accessibility issues with using the iPad keyboard. It is an app that recognizes speech and converts it into text. It also has a facility for copying, pasting and deleting text that has been created.

- **GoSkyWatch.** Astronomy apps are some of the most popular for the iPad. This one takes account of your own geographical location and then determines the makeup of the stars and planets when you point the iPad camera towards the sky. You can then tap on the items on the screen to find out more information about them.

- **iTouchiLearn.** Two apps for pre-school children, one for words and one for numbers. They provide games and activities that help with reading, writing, spelling and counting.

- **iWriteWords.** Another reading and writing app for pre-school children that enables them to trace letters following a specific path on the screen.

- **Math Ninja.** A mathematics app for pre-school children that allows them to adopt a Ninja character to complete multiple choice tasks in adding, subtracting, multiplication and division.

- **Mental Case 2.** This is another powerful flashcard app, with high quality graphics. There are pre-designed flashcards and you can also create your own, with text, audio and images.

- **My First Words — Flashcards by Alligator Apps.** An app containing flashcards for pre-school children. You can create your own cards and update existing ones. It is fully customizable and in addition to the flashcards themselves, there are also games to help make learning fun.

- **NASA.** This is another popular astronomy app, with a host of information and images of planets, stars and general information about NASA and space exploration.

- **Pearl Diver.** An interactive mathematics app developed by educators, researchers and game developers. It takes place in a deep sea environment. It is appropriate for middle school or primary school level.

- **Rocket Math.** Similar to Pearl Diver, but the games and quizzes take place in a space environment. It contains different categories that are appropriate for children of all ages and levels of ability.

...cont'd

- **Solar Walk.** An astronomy app that enables you to explore, and learn about, the solar system in 3D.

- **Solar System Journey.** An in-depth app, that explains everything about the solar system that you probably ever wanted to know.

- **Stack the States.** Similar to the Stack the Countries geography app, but for the States in the USA.

- **StoryKit.** An innovative writing and reading app that enables you to create your own stories. These can be based on existing books, or you can create them from scratch.

- **Strip Designer.** For the artistically inclined, this is an app for creating your own cartoon strips. You can use your own photos and then add text balloons and graphics.

- **TED.** This is an app that will appeal to anyone who is interested in learning and asking questions. TED stands for Technology, Entertainment and Design and the app contains a range of stimulating and challenging talks and lectures on a range of diverse subjects:

- **Toontastic.** Another creative app, for budding animators. You can draw your own cartoons and then animate them in a game-based environment. The finished animations can also be shared with other people.

6 iPad for Productivity

When the iPad was first released, questions were asked about how effective it would be in terms of productivity. However, this chapter shows how these issues have been addressed by a range of apps that cover productivity, from word processing to organizational tasks such as homework apps and flashcards for revision.

Productivity on the iPad

When the iPad was first introduced the initial reaction from a lot of people was that it would be great for entertainment and communications, but how would it manage with more prosaic productivity tasks such as word processing and creating and saving documents? For parents and teachers, this is an important issue since they will want their children to use the iPad as more than just an entertainment tool. But due to the versatility of the iPad, and the wealth of productivity apps that have been developed, it can now be viewed as a genuine productivity tool. Some of the productivity possibilities that there are for the iPad are:

Don't forget

Generally, productivity apps save your work as you create it so you do not have to keep remembering to constantly select Save.

- Word processing

- Presentations

- Spreadsheets

- Reference material, including books and journals

- Organizational apps, such as note-taking

It's all in the apps

As with most things to do with the iPad, it is the apps that make productivity possible. There is a productivity category within the App Store where there is a range of apps for creating, and viewing, content.

The built-in Newsstand app can also be used to store books and magazines which can be used for productivity purposes.

Saving Your Work

For anyone who has grown up with computers and is used to a clear file structure, the first question when faced with an iPad is sometimes, 'Where do I save things?'. Unlike a Windows PC with File Explorer, or a Mac with the Finder, there is no obvious place to save files or create folders for content. This is because there isn't one. So where do you save your essays, presentations or photos once they have been created?

Self-contained saving

Instead of having a separate structure into which you can save files, content is saved within the apps in which they are created. So, if you write an essay with the Pages word processing app, this is where it will be saved, and similarly if you create a presentation within the Keynote app. Documents can be viewed as follows:

1 Tap once on the **Documents** button

| Documents |

2 All saved documents can be viewed here

3 When new documents are created they are added to this section. This is essentially the top level folder

The button in Step 1 will usually be relevant to the type of app, e.g. for the Keynote presentation app, the button is Presentations, but the process is the same.

111

A lot of apps from Apple are linked to iCloud so your work can be stored and shared here.

...cont'd

Adding folders

Despite the lack of a folder structure within the iPad operating system, folders can be created within some productivity apps, such as Pages. To do this:

1 Tap and hold on a document until it starts to jiggle. Drag it over another document icon

2 The new folder is created. Tap once here to give it a relevant name, then tap anywhere outside the folder to finish, or tap once on **Done** on the keyboard, or on the top toolbar

Beware

You cannot create sub-folders, i.e. folders within folders. So the folder structure can only go down one level.

3 The new folder appears in the main document area next to existing files

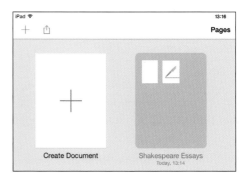

Printing Your Work

Printing from an iPad has advantages and disadvantages. The advantage is that it is done wirelessly so you do not have to worry about connecting wires and cables to a printer. The disadvantage is that there's a limited number of printers that work with the iPad printing system, although this number is going up all the time.

AirPrint

Content from an iPad is printed using the AirPrint system that is part of the iOS operating system. This is a wireless printing system that connects to your printer through your Wi-Fi network. However, not all printers are AirPrint-enabled so it may not work with your current printer.

AirPrint can print content from Safari, Mail, Photos, Pages, Keynote, Numbers and PDF documents in iBooks. Some third-party apps have AirPrint facilities but this depends on individual developers. To print items using AirPrint:

Check on the Apple website for a list of AirPrint-enabled printers.

1 Tap once on the tools button

2 Tap once on the **Print** link

Some developers offer third-party printing apps, which work with varying degrees of success.

3 Select a printer or, if it has already been set up, tap once on the **Print** button to print

4 If your printer is not AirPrint compatible this will be shown in the Printer dialog box

Pages

Pages is a word processing app for the iPad and also other Mac computers and mobile devices. It is created by Apple and is part of the iWork suite of apps that also includes Keynote for presentations and Numbers for spreadsheets.

Pages is a powerful word processor for a mobile device and although it does not have the same range of features as the version for desktop or laptop computers, it is more than capable of producing high quality documents.

Creating documents

Once you have downloaded the Pages app, documents can be created as follows:

Don't forget

Documents created in Pages on the iPad can be shared on other devices that have Pages. However, if you have Pages on an iMac or MacBook you will still have to buy the iPad version separately.

114

Hot tip

Since Pages is an Apple app you can be confident that it will be fully supported for the iPad and also developed and updated on a regular basis.

1 Tap once on this icon

2 Tap once on this button to create a new document, or

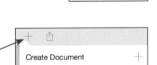

3 Tap once here and tap on the **Create Document** button

4 Pages comes with a range of pre-designed templates that can be used as the basis of your document. Tap once on a template to select it for your document. All elements of a template can be replaced with your own content

5 The document is created, based on the selected template. (If the **Blank** template is selected, there will be no content in the document)

Pages documents are saved automatically as you work on them.

6 Tap once on the **Documents** button to view the document in the Pages folder environment

Documents

7 The document appears here in the folder area

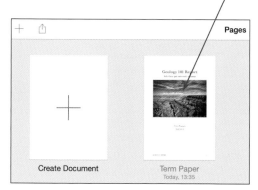

Create Document

Term Paper
Today, 13:35

To delete a document, tap and hold on it until it starts to jiggle. Then tap once on the waste bin icon on the toolbar and tap once on the **Delete Document** link that appears in red.

8 Tap once on the file name and type a new name as required and tap once on the **Done** button

Done

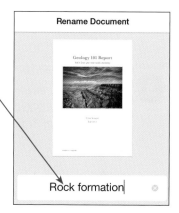

Rename Document

Rock formation

...cont'd

Formatting text

Once a new document has been created, content can be added to it. To do this:

Options for using
the iPad keyboard in
different configurations
are shown in
Chapter Two.

1 Tap once on the new document and use the keyboard to add text. Tap once on the buttons on the bottom toolbar to format selected text

2 Tap once on these buttons to, from left to right, tab selected text and change the font

3 Tap once on these buttons to, from left to right, change the size of selected text, add bold, italics or underlining and align text

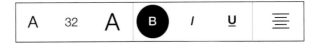

Selecting text

In order to perform the formatting on the previous page, text has to first be selected. Text also has to be selected if you want to copy and paste it.

Text can be selected in this way across most iPad apps and also on web pages.

1 To change the insertion point, tap and hold until the magnifying glass appears

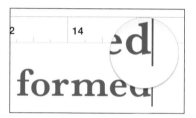

2 Drag the magnifying glass to move the insertion point

Once the selection buttons have been accessed, tap once on **Select** to select the previous word, or **Select All** to select all text.

3 Tap once at the insertion point to access the selection buttons

4 Double-tap on a word to select it. Tap once on **Cut** or **Copy** as required

5 Drag the selection handles to expand or contract the selection

6 If text has been copied, tap and hold at a new point on the page and tap once on **Paste**

...cont'd

Adding media

With Pages you can add a variety of different types of content, in addition to text. One of the most commonly-used types of media in word processing documents are images. To add these in Pages:

1 Tap once here and tap once on the Media button. Tap once on a location on your iPad from which to select an image. Navigate to this and tap once on an image to add it to the document

Hot tip

Images can be incorporated with text in different ways using the **Wrap** option from the **Arrange** button in Step 3. The options are **Automatic**, **Around** and, **Above and Below**. There is also a button that can be dragged to **On** so that the image moves with the text.

2 Tap once on an image to select it. Drag the placeholder buttons to resize the image

3 With an image selected, tap once on this button to access editing options for the image. Tap once on the **Edit Mask** button to crop the image

Hot tip

The Mask option can also be accessed by double-tapping on an image in a document.

4 Drag the resizing handles to select the area you want to keep. Tap once on the **Done** button to complete the operation

118

...cont'd

Other elements that can be added within Pages are:

1 Tap once on the same button as for images and tap once on the **Tables** button to add pre-designed tables. Tap once on a table to add it to a document. Tap once to select it in a document and resize it in the same way as an image

2 Tap once on the **Charts** button to add pre-designed charts. Tap once on a chart to add it to a document. Tap once to select it in a document. Once it is selected, tap once on **Edit Data**, (above the chart) to add your own data

Hot tip

To move through the pages of the Tables, Charts and Shapes sections, tap once on the small dots at the bottom of the window.

3 Tap once on the **Shapes** button to add pre-designed shapes. Tap once on a shape to add it to a document. Tap once to select it in a document and resize it in the same way as an image

...cont'd

Tools and Settings

To access additional tools and settings options:

1 Tap once on this button on the toolbar

Don't forget

Tap once on the **Document Setup** link to access a page from where you can set page margins and add headers and footers.

2 The available tools are for **Find** (for finding items in a document), **Change Tracking**, **Document Setup**, **Settings**, **Set Password**, **Print** and general **Help** information

Hot tip

When you email a document from Pages (using the **Share** button and **Send a Copy**) there are options for saving it in a Pages, PDF or Word format.

3 Tap once on the **Settings** link to access options for this. This includes activating the spell checker and the word count and also options for setting guidelines on a page

Don't forget

The **Share** button can be used in all of the iWork apps: Pages, Keynote and Numbers.

4 Tap once on this button to access the **Share** options, including sharing a document via iCloud so that you can access it from other iCloud-enabled devices

Keynote

Keynote is another app in Apple's iWork suite. It is used for creating presentations, in a similar style to the Microsoft PowerPoint program. It can be used to make individual slides and also slideshow presentations with multiple slides.

Creating presentations
To create presentations in Keynote:

Keynote is an excellent app for school projects and also for giving talks to classmates.

1 Tap once on this icon

2 Tap once on this button to create a new presentation, or

Create Presentation

3 Tap once here and tap on the **Create Presentation** button

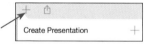
Create Presentation

4 Tap once on a template to select it for the first slide of your presentation

New presentations are stored in the same way as with Pages documents and folders can also be created in the same way.

5 The content of the template forms the basis for the first slide of your presentation. This can now be edited with your own content. (In some cases there may be more content in the template slides when you add new slides, see page 125)

DOUBLE-TAP TO EDIT

...cont'd

Adding content

The main elements of slides in Keynote are images and text. These can be added by editing the existing content that is provided by some of the templates. To do this:

If you select a blank template, i.e. a white, black or gradient one, it will still have a placeholder for text and placeholders for images can be added with subsequent slides.

Double-tap on an image to access the mask option for cropping parts of the image.

1 Tap once on an image to select it and tap once on this icon on the image or on the toolbar

2 Select a new image in the same way as for Pages. If an image is already selected in the slide it will be replaced by the new one. If nothing is selected the image will be inserted

3 Tap once here and tap once on the **Style** button to select styles for the appearance of the image

4 Tap once as above and tap once on the **Arrange** button to select options for how the image appears in relation to other objects, its orientation and mask options for cropping

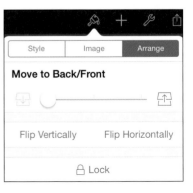

To add and format text:

1 Double-tap on the placeholder text to add your own

2 Enter text with the keyboard

Don't forget

When you select a text box you automatically have options to **Cut**, **Copy** or **Delete** it.

3 Resize the text by dragging the resizing handles or hold and drag to move the whole text box

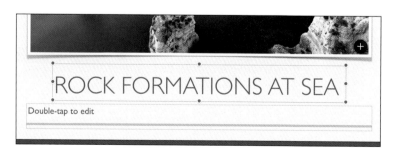

...cont'd

4 Tap once here and tap on the **Style** button to select a style for the selected text. This includes drop shadows and a colored background behind the text. Tap once on the **Style Options** link to access more options

5 From the **Style Options**, select a color for the text. Tap once on the **Border** and **Effects** buttons to access more options

6 Tap once as above in Step 4 and tap on the **Text** button to select formatting options and also pre-designed styles that can be applied to the text box

Drag the **Move to Back/Front** button to change the order of a text box in relation to other objects, such as images.

7 Tap once as above in Step 4 and tap on the **Arrange** button to select options for how the text appears in relation to other objects and alignment options

Adding slides

Once you have created your first slide you can then add more to build up your presentation. To do this:

1 Tap once here and select a new style for the subsequent slide. This can either be the same as the first slide or it can be a new style. Tap once on a slide to add it to the presentation

To delete a slide, tap on it once to select it in the left-hand panel. Tap on it once again and tap once on the **Delete** button that appears.

2 The new slide is shown in the presentation here. Enter content in the same way as for the first slide

...cont'd

Animations and Transitions

One of the most eye-catching features of presentation apps is their ability to apply animated effects to objects and slides. Animations can be applied to images or text within individual slides. This determines how they are introduced and removed from the slide. To do this:

Beware

Do not use too many Build In and Build Out effects. Otherwise the slide may become too 'busy' and distracting for the viewer.

1 Tap once on this button on the toolbar to access the animation options

2 Tap once on an item in a slide to select it. This activates the Build In and Build Out buttons

3 Tap once for the **Build In** option. Select an option for how the object is animated into the slide. Repeat the process for the **Build Out** effect, if required. Tap on the **Play** button to preview the effect

Beware

Keep objects together if you are reordering them, i.e. do not split up an image and a text box.

4 When animations have been added this is denoted on the object by these icons

5 In the Build In or Build Out window, tap once on the **Order** button at the bottom and drag an item up or down to change the order of the animated effects for each object on the slide

To create transition effects between slides:

1 Tap once on this button on the toolbar to access the transition options

2 Tap once on one of the slides in the left-hand panel. Tap once here to add a transition

3 Tap once on a transition effect

To return to the Home screen tap once on the **Done** button, once you have added animations and transitions.

4 Tap once on a slide to view the transition effect that has been applied to it

5 Tap once on this button on the toolbar to preview the slideshow. This can be done at any point during the creation of the presentation

When previewing a presentation, tap once to move to the next effect on a slide, or to move to the next slide.

ROCK FORMATIONS AT SEA

Numbers

Numbers is the spreadsheet app in the iWork suite. It is used for creating spreadsheets containing plain text and also formula with tables of figures.

Creating spreadsheets

To create spreadsheets in Numbers:

1 Tap once on this icon

2 Tap once on this button to create a new spreadsheet, or

Don't forget

There are other spreadsheets available in the App Store but Numbers is one of the most powerful, flexible and versatile.

3 Tap once here and tap on the **Create Spreadsheet** button

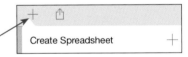

4 Tap once on a template to select it for the spreadsheet. If you want to create your own spreadsheet from scratch, tap once on the **Blank** template

5 The spreadsheet is saved into the folder area in the same way as with Pages documents and Keynote presentations

Adding content

Content can be added to cells of a spreadsheet in Numbers in different formats. These are:

- Numbers

- Date

- Text

- Formulae

To add content:

1 Double-tap on a cell to access the input options

2 Tap once here to enter numbers with the keypad

3 Tap once here to add a date or duration format, using the buttons to the right. Use the keypad to enter a specific day

4 Tap once here to enter text with the keypad

Tap once on a cell to select it, rather than double-tapping for the input options. Once it is selected, formatting options can be applied.

Tap once on the **Done** button once you have input the required items.

129

...cont'd

Adding formulae

The ability to add formulae to cells is a vital part of the functionality of a spreadsheet app as it enables the app to perform calculations with the data that has been added. To do this:

1 Tap once here to enter a formula for a cell

Beware

Formulae in a Numbers spreadsheet can be as simple or as complicated as you like. The most common ones are **Sum** and **Average**, but you can add more complex functions and also add your own manually by typing it in the formula bar next to the function.

2 Tap once on the **Functions** button to access the different available types of formulae. Tap once on one to select it

3 Tap once on a cell and drag over consecutive cells to add them to the formula as a group. This is added next to the selected formula

4 Tap once on individual cells to add them to the formula as individual items.
This can be used to add non-consecutive items, if required

5 Tap once on the green button to accept a formula and the red button to reject it

Formatting content

Content within individual cells of a spreadsheet can be formatted, as can the spreadsheet as a whole. To do this:

1 Tap once on a cell to select it

2 Tap once here and tap once on the **Table** button. Tap once on a formatting option for the style of the spreadsheet

3 Tap once on the **Table Options** button to access more formatting options for the table

4 Tap once on the **Headers** button to select options for the spreadsheet's headers and footers

Don't forget

Table options can be set for the table name, showing or hiding the table border, different shades for alternating rows, options for formatting the table grid and font options that apply to all text within the table.

...cont'd

Within the **Cells** section, tap once on the **Text Options** link to access options for editing the size, color and font of the text in a selected cell.

132

Under the **Share > Send a Copy** option, a spreadsheet can be emailed in a Numbers, PDF or Excel format.

5 Tap once on the **Cells** button to select formatting options for the selected cell

6 Tap once on the **Format** button to select formatting options for the content of the selected cell, e.g. to show figures as numbers, currency or percentages. Each option has additional settings to refine the selection, e.g. adding decimal places for numbers

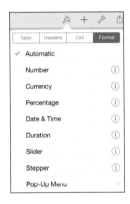

7 Tap once here to add content in the same way as for Pages and Keynote, i.e. photos, tables, charts and shapes

8 Tap once here to **Find** items in the spreadsheet, access Numbers **Settings**, **Set Password**, **Print** the spreadsheet, and general **Help**

Adding and editing sheets

Within a spreadsheet it is possible to add sheets, move the sheet on which you are working, resize it and edit the size of rows and columns. To do this:

1 Tap once here to add a new sheet

Hot tip

Cells can be expanded by dragging to accommodate text. Text can also be wrapped in a cell by selecting the **Wrap Text in Cell** option within the **Cells** section.

2 Tap once on a cell to select it and drag on this button to move the spreadsheet

3 Drag on this button to resize the spreadsheet

Hot tip

When a column is selected there are options for cutting, copying or deleting it, inserting another column, sorting its contents, fitting the column to the contents, hiding the column and creating a chart from its contents.

4 Tap once on a cell to select it and then tap here to select a column (or row if selected vertically). Drag to resize the selected item

iBooks

iBooks is an app that enables you to access, download and read books and educational textbooks. It has a similar interface to the App Store and the iTunes Store, so it should be familiar to anyone who has used these. The iBooks app can initially be downloaded from within the App Store. To do this:

1 Access the iBooks app in the App Store and download it in the same way as for other apps

2 Tap once on this icon once the **iBooks** app has been downloaded

Hot tip

The range of books within the iBooks Store is suitable for all ages, including adults.

3 The iBooks app interface consists of a bookcase, which is empty initially. Tap once on the **Store** button to access the iBooks store

4 Navigate through the iBooks Store in the same way as the App Store to find the required titles

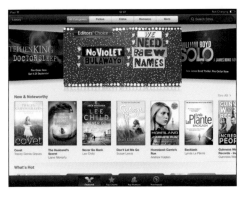

5 Use these buttons to search for items within the iBooks Store

Downloading books

Once you have identified appropriate books they can then be
downloaded to the iBooks bookcase. To do this:

1 Tap once on the book name or title to view its details

2 Review the details of the book and view sample pages. Tap once here to download the book

Don't forget

The iBooks bookcase is also known as the Library. Use these buttons at the top right-hand side of the toolbar to view the content by icon or text. Tap once on the **Edit** button to delete an item, by tapping on it once and then tapping once on the **Delete** button.

3 Downloaded books appear on the iBooks bookcase. Tap once on a book cover to open it

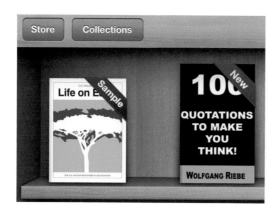

...cont'd

Reading an iBook
Once you have opened an iBook:

1 Tap once on a page in an iBook to access the top toolbar

Swipe left or right to move between pages within an iBook.

2 Tap once on these buttons to, from left to right, change the brightness, search for items or bookmark a page

3 Tap once on this button to view the Table of Contents and the Glossary (if there is one)

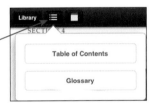

4 Tap once on this button to access a page where you can enter your own notes

5 Tap once here to add your own notes or to highlight a piece of text

Finding textbooks

Within iBooks there is a range of textbooks that can be used for schoolwork. To find these:

1 Enter the relevant keywords in the **iBooks Store Search box,** based on the subject of the textbook

2 Tap once on a title to review its contents. Tap once on the **Free** button to download it

3 Navigate through the book contents by tapping once to access the main toolbar. Swipe left or right to move between pages

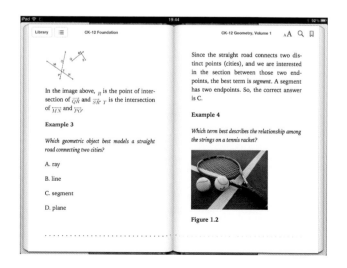

Newsstand

Newsstand is a built-in iPad app that is similar to iBooks, except that it deals with magazines, newspapers and journals rather than books. To use Newsstand:

1 Tap once on this icon

2 The Newsstand bookcase is initially empty. Tap once on the Store button to access the Newsstand Store

Store

Don't forget

For a lot of items within the Newsstand it is free to download a sample version but you then need to pay a subscription for the selected newspaper, journal or magazine.

3 The Newsstand Store is incorporated within the App Store. Items can be found in the same way as with other items in the App Store

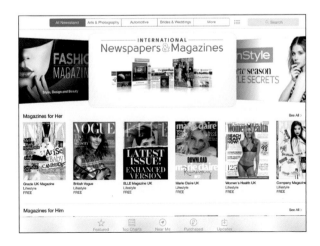

4 When you have found a suitable magazine, newspaper or journal, review and download it in the same way as with an app or an iBook

Most items within the Newsstand are better suited to older children.

5 Downloaded items appear on the Newsstand bookcase (Library). Tap once on a cover to open that publication

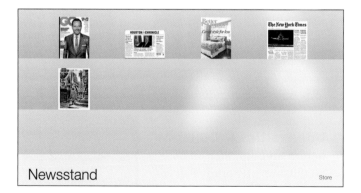

6 Tap once on a page to access the top toolbar. This contains items for accessing the Homepage of the publication, a contents page and options for zooming and sharing a page via email, Facebook or to a Photo Album

iTunes U

For older students, and also adults interested in further education, the iTunes U app provides access to a wide range of courses from universities and schools around the world. This is a fantastic resource, made all the better by the fact that the majority of courses are free. To use iTunes U:

1 Access the iTunes U app in the App Store and download it

2 Tap once on the **Catalog** button to access the iTunes U catalog of courses

Different establishments have their own style for presenting their material.

3 The courses within iTunes U can be accessed from the Homepage

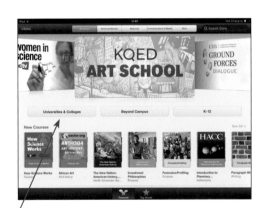

4 Tap once on the **Universities & Colleges** button and tap once on an establishment from which you would like to view their range of courses

5 Navigate from the Homepage of the selected establishment to find their courses

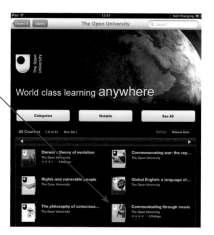

6 Tap once on the **Subscribe** button to download the course material

If there is supplementary material for the course, this will be shown by a blue circle at the top right-hand corner of the course cover on the iTunes U bookcase.

7 The selected course is downloaded to the iTunes U bookcase. Tap once on a cover to access the course content

8 Swipe through the pages to view the course content and use the tabs down the right-hand side to view additional items such as notes pages and further information

Keeping Organized

Parents and teachers always want their children and pupils to try to be as organized as possible when approaching their school work. With the iPad this can now all be done digitally rather than having to rely on hard copy diaries and timetables. There are various types of apps that can help with this:

- **Homework apps.** These are apps that act in a similar way to a traditional school timetable. Classes and items of homework can be added to act as a mobile reminder about school work and activities

- **General organization apps,** such as note taking, calendars and address books

- **Flashcard apps.** These are apps for creating your own reminders for revision for specific subjects

MyHomework

This is representative of homework apps. To use this:

Hot tip

A lot of homework apps have an online facility. This means that you can log in to the app and once you have registered you can then access your homework information from a web browser or through Facebook.

1 Tap once on this icon

2 Tap once on this button to show and hide the main toolbar on any page to return to the Home screen

3 Tap once on these icons to return to the Home screen, access the homework calendar, add new homework items or view information that has been added by teachers

4 Tap once on the plus sign next to **Classes**

5 Tap once on **Add a Class Manually** button

6 Enter the subjects and times for the required school classes. Tap once on the **Save** button to create the classes

7 Tap once on the **Home** button and tap once on the plus sign next to **Homework**

8 Enter the homework topic and when it is due. Tap once on the **Save** button to create the homework item

9 The item is added to the Homework section

Reminders can be set for homework items, but this sometimes requires an online account, depending on the app.

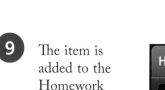

Tap once on the **Calendar** button on the toolbar to view classes or homework that is due for a specific date.

143

...cont'd

Evernote

This is one of the most popular note-taking apps. It is available on the iPad and there are also versions for the iPhone and desktop PCs and laptops (for both Mac OS X and Windows). This means that whatever you add to Evernote, it will be synchronized and available over all of your devices. Notes in Evernote on the iPad can be created with text, audio and photos. To use Evernote:

Don't forget

Once you have created an Evernote account you can use the login details to view your Evernote account on any mobile device or computer with Internet access.

1 Tap once on this icon

2 Tap once on the **Create Account** button. This enables you to create your Evernote account so that you can access your information from different sources. This is free. When you have an account, tap once on the **Sign In** button to sign in with your username and password

3 The Home screen contains a panel down the left-hand side for accessing your content. Tap once on the **Notes** heading to view your notes and start creating new ones

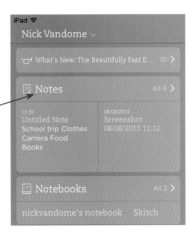

4 To create a new note, tap once on this button

5 Enter details for the new note. Use the buttons at the top to add audio and photos to the note and also take a photo with the iPad for the note. Use the bottom toolbar to format the text in the note. Tap once on the **Save** button once you have finished the note

6 The note appears in the **Notes** area. Tap once on it to edit it

Hot tip

The desktop/laptop version of Evernote enables you to view PDF files and capture areas of web pages (known as a Web Clipper).

7 On the Home screen use these quick link buttons to create new note, take photos, access your media and set alerts

Calendars

The iPad has a built-in Calendar app that can be used to note appointments for social events and also school work. To use the Calendar app:

Swipe up and down to move between dates in the Calendar app. The months can be viewed with continuous scrolling, which means you can view weeks across two months in the same window (if the calendar is in month view).

To edit an event, tap on it and tap on the **Edit** button. Amend the details in the **Edit** window. To delete the event, swipe down to the bottom of the **Edit** window and tap on the **Delete Event** button.

1 Tap once on this icon

2 Use these buttons to view the calendar in different formats

3 Tap once on a day, week, month or year, or

4 Tap once on the **Today** button in the bottom left-hand corner to view the calendar for the current date

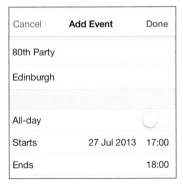

5 Tap and hold on a time slot to add a new event

6 Enter details of the event and tap once on the **Done** button

Address Books

Children usually have a lot of friends and contacts so it is useful to have somewhere where their details can be recorded and saved. For parents this can also be useful if they need to get in touch with their child's friends. On the iPad the Contacts app serves as an address book. To use this:

1 Tap once on this icon

Your contacts can be used in a selection of apps, including Mail, Game Center, FaceTime and Messages.

2 Tap once on this button to add a new contact

3 Enter the details for the new contact

4 Tap once on the **Done** button

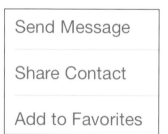

5 The contact is added to the address book. Use these buttons to contact them via text or video messaging or share their details with someone else or add them to your favorite contacts

Send Message

Share Contact

Add to Favorites

There is also a built-in **Reminders** app that can be used to create specific reminders, which can be set to appear in the Notification Center.

6 Select a contact and tap once on the **Edit** button to edit their details

Edit

Flashcards

Flashcards are revision aids that come with information already inserted on them and you can also make up your own flashcards for specific subjects. Flashcard apps are similar in their functionality. The examples here are for the Flashcards app:

1 Tap once on this icon

2 On the Home screen, tap once on the **add deck** button, in the bottom right-hand corner

3 Tap once on the **Search Decks** button and select a source location

The content for the flashcards is essentially a database of information. Once it is downloaded it is converted into the flashcard format.

4 Tap once on one of the main categories. Navigate to a topic and tap once on it to view the flashcard content

5 The content (questions and answers) is displayed

6 If you want to use these flashcards, tap once on the **Download** button

7 This will download the content to a deck of flashcards within the **Decks** area. Tap once on a deck name to access the relevant flashcards

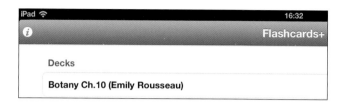

8 The question is displayed on the front of the flashcard

9 Swipe left or right to view the answer on the reverse of the flashcard

Although you can edit the pre-designed flashcards, make sure that you do not change anything that makes them incorrect.

10 Tap once on the tick to move to the next flashcard. Tap once on **edit card** to change the card

11 Tap on the screen and tap once on the button in the top left-hand corner to go back up to the top level of the deck of flashcards

...cont'd

Creating your own flashcards

In addition to the pre-designed flashcards it is also possible to create decks of your own flashcards. To do this:

Don't forget

The question above the line in Step 3 becomes the front of the flashcard and the answer below it becomes the back.

1 On the Home screen, tap once on the **Add Deck** button and tap once on the **Add Custom Deck** button

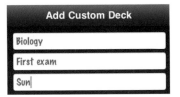

2 Enter a Deck Name, Deck Subject and Deck Description. Tap once on the **Save** button

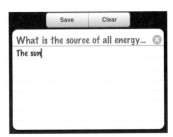

3 Enter the question above the red line and the answer below it. Tap once on the **Save** button

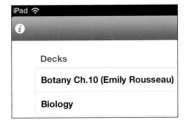

4 On the Home screen tap once on the deck name under the **Decks** heading

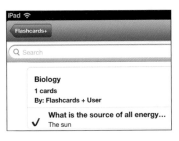

5 Tap once on a deck to view its flashcards

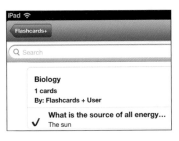

7 Photos and Videos

With the proliferation of mobile devices such as the iPad, it has never been easier for children to create and share photos and videos. This chapter shows how to use the Photos app for working with images and the iMovie app for editing video.

Using the Camera

Because of its mobility and the quality of the screen, the iPad is excellent for taking and displaying photos. Photos can be captured directly using one of the two built-in cameras (one on the front and one on the back) and then viewed, edited and shared using the Photos app. To do this:

Don't forget

The front camera on the iPad is an iSight 5 megapixel device. This is capable of capturing high-quality images and also HD videos.

1 Tap once on the Camera app

2 Tap once on this button to capture a photo

3 Tap once on this button to swap between the front or back cameras on the iPad

Camera Settings
Certain camera options can be applied within Settings:

Hot tip

Photos that are captured with the iPad camera are saved in the **Camera Roll** within the **Albums** section of the **Photos** app, as well as in the main Photos area.

1 Tap once on the **Settings** app

2 Tap once on the **Photos & Camera** tab

3 Drag the **Photo Sharing** button to On to enable sharing via a photo stream (see page 154)

4 Drag the **Grid** button to On to

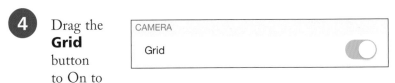

place a grid over the screen, if required. This can be used to help compose photos by placing subjects using the grid

Taking Photos

Photos taken with the camera on the iPad can be done in standard format or square format.

1 Swipe up or down at the side of the camera screen, underneath the shutter button. Tap once on the **Photo** button to capture photos at full screen size

Be careful to keep your fingers away from the camera lens when you are taking photos, particularly when you are using the camera on the other side of the iPad.

2 Swipe up or down at the side of the camera screen, underneath the shutter button. Tap once on the **Square** button to capture photos at this ratio

Tap once on the HDR (High Dynamic Range) button to take three versions of the same subject that will then be blended into a single photo, using the best exposures from each photo.

Viewing Photos

Once photos have been captured they can be viewed and organized in the Photos app. To do this:

If you have iCloud set up, all of your photos will also be saved under the **My Photo Stream** button in the **Albums** section. This enables all of your photos to be made available on any other iCloud-enabled devices.

1 Tap once on the **Photos** app

2 At the top level, all photos are displayed according to the years in which they were taken

Don't forget

Tap once on the **Photos**, **Shared** and **Albums** buttons at the bottom of the **Years**, **Collections** or **Moments** windows, to view the photos in each of these sections.

3 Tap once within the **Years** window to view photos according to specific, more defined, timescales. This is the **Collections** level. Tap once on the **Years** button to move back up one level

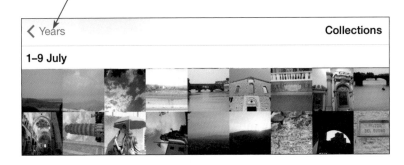

4 Tap once within the **Collections** window to drill down further into the photos, within the **Moments** window. Tap once on the **Collections** button to go back up one level

Moments are created according to the time at which the photos were added or taken: photos added at the same time will be displayed within the same Moment.

5 Tap once on a photo within the **Moments** window to view it at full size. Tap once on the **Moments** button to go back up one level

Double-tap with one finger on an individual photo to zoom in on it. Double-tap with one finger again to zoom back out. To zoom in to a greater degree, swipe outwards with thumb and forefinger.

6 Swipe with one finger or drag here to move through all of the available photos in a specific Moment

Creating Albums

Within the Photo app it is possible to create different albums in which you can store photos. This can be a good way to organize them according to different categories and headings. To do this:

When photos are placed into albums the originals remain in the main **Photos** section.

1 Tap once on the **Albums** button

Albums

2 Tap once on this button

3 Enter a name for the new album

New Album
Enter a name for this album.

Italy

Cancel | Save

Albums can be viewed as slideshows. To do this open the album and tap once on the **Slideshow** button.

Slideshow

Make the required selections and tap once on the **Start Slideshow** button.

4 Tap once on the **Save** button

5 Tap on the photos you want to include in the album

Moments | Done
Add 3 photos to "Italy".
Select

6 Tap once on the **Done** button

Done

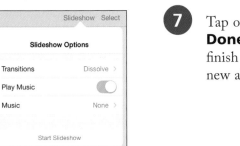

Slideshow Select

Slideshow Options

Transitions | Dissolve >
Play Music
Music | None >

Start Slideshow

7 Tap once on the **Done** button to finish creating the new album

Done

Done

Italy

Selecting Photos

It is easy to take hundreds, or thousands, of digital photos and most of the time you will only want to use a selection of them. Within the Photos app it is possible to select individual photos so that you can share them, delete them or add them to albums.

1 Access the Moments section and tap once on **Select** button

Select

Hot tip

Press and hold on a photo to access an option to copy it, rather than selecting it.

2 Tap on the photos you want to select, or tap once on the **Select** button again to select all of the photos

Don't forget

To add items to an album, tap once on this button in the **Moments** section.

Select

Tap once on photos to select them, then tap once on the **Add To** button and select either an existing album or tap once on the **New Album** link to create a new album with the selected photos added to it.

3 Tap once on the **Deselect** button if you want to remove the selection

4 Use these buttons to, from left to right, share the selected photos, delete them or add them to an album

Add To

Sharing Photos

Within the Photos app there are a number of ways to share and use photos. To do this:

1 Open a photo at full size and tap once on this button

2 Tap once on one of the options for sharing the photo. These include messaging, emailing, sending to iCloud, adding to a contact in your Contacts app, using as your iPad wallpaper, tweeting, sending to Facebook or Flickr, printing and copying the photo

Sharing Moments
Photo Moments can also be shared:

1 Access the **Moments** section and tap once on the **Share** button

2 Select **Share this moment** to share all of the photos in the moment, or **Share some photos** to make a selection

3 Select one of the sharing options (there may be fewer options when sharing multiple photos)

Tweeting is done on the social networking site, Twitter.

Sharing with Photo Stream

The Photo Stream option can be used to share photos with other people with the iCloud Photo Stream sharing function. To use this:

1 Select photos you want to share via Photo Stream and tap on the **Share** button

2 Tap once on the **iCloud** button

3 Enter a name for the new Photo Stream and tap once on the **Next** button

4 Enter a recipient with whom you want to share the Photo Stream and tap once on the **Create** button

5 Tap once on the **Next** button and enter a comment about the Photo Stream. Tap once on the **Post** button

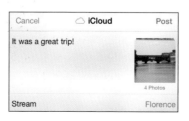

Hot tip

Once a Photo Stream has been posted, the recipient receives an email inviting them to view it.

Editing Photos

Children enjoy editing and changing photos and the Photos app has options to perform some basic photo-editing operations.

1 Open a photo at full-screen size and tap once on the **Edit** button

2 Tap once on the **Rotate** button to rotate the photo 90 degrees at a time, anti-clockwise

3 Tap once on the **Enhance** button to have auto-coloring editing applied to the photo

4 Tap once on the **Filters** button to select special effects to be applied to the photo

5 Tap once on the **Crop** button and drag the resizing handles to select an area of the photo that you want to keep, and discard the rest

Most photos benefit from some cropping, to enhance the main subject and give it greater prominence.

6 For each function, tap once on the **Save** button to save the photo with the selected changes

7 Tap once on these buttons to, from left to right, Cancel the whole editing process, Undo the editing changes one step at a time, and remove all of the changes and go back to the original photo

Creative Photo Effects

As well as editing and sharing photos there are a number of fun creative effects that can be achieved. This is done with the Photo Booth app. To do this:

1 Tap once on this icon

Photo Booth

2 The different special effects are shown through the camera. Tap once to select the desired effect

3 Review the image and capture it in the same way as for any other photo

Capturing Video

The iPad cameras can also be used to capture video, as well as photos. To do this:

1 Tap once on the **Camera** app

2 Swipe up or down so that the **Video** button is highlighted

3 Tap once on this button to swap cameras from front to back

Don't forget

The built-in iPad **Videos** app is used for storing videos that are downloaded from iTunes, rather than the ones that are captured with the iPad camera.

4 Tap once on this button to record a video. Tap once on it again to stop recording

5 Once a video has been captured it is saved within the Photos app with the video camera icon and the duration of the video showing on the thumbnail. Tap once on this button to play a video

Editing Video

Once video has been captured it can then be edited to produce a more stylish final product. This cannot be done with any of the built-in iPad apps but there are video editing apps that can be downloaded from the App Store. The most popular is Apple's own iMovie. To use this:

1. Tap once on this icon

2. Within the iMovie interface tap once on the **Projects** button and tap here to start a new video project

Video   Projects   Theater

3. Tap once on the **Movie** option to create and edit your own movie

4. Select a template for your movie and tap once on the **Create Movie** button

5 Available video clips are displayed here. Tap once on a video clip to select it and tap once on this button to add the clip to the timeline for editing

Tap once on this button to access **Help** options within iMovie.

6 The video clip is added to the iMovie editing window

Preview window   Video clips for downloading

The Preview window plays the edited video project on the Timeline.

Timeline, where the video project is created and edited. Drag the clip left or right to move it over the Playhead (the white line)

7 Tap once on this button to capture more video content and add it to the project

...cont'd

Adding content

Once video clips have been added, your video project can be added to and edited in a number of ways. To do this:

1 Tap once on the **Photos** tab to add photos to your project

2 Tap once on the **Audio** tab to add a range of music and audio effects

3 Tap once on a video clip on the timeline to access the edit and content options. These include adding a **Title**, changing the **Speed**, **Splitting** the clip, **Freezing** the clip or **Deleting** the clip

4 Tap once on the **Title** option in Step 3 to add text to the video clip. Select an option for where it is added

Titles appear over the length of a clip. If you want to create opening and closing titles, split the video clips at the beginning and end of the project.

5 Enter a title here and tap once on this button on the bottom toolbar to format the text

Title Text Here

T

Video clips can also be split by swiping downwards over the playhead. Once a clip has been split the two new clips can be edited separately. They can also be reordered by dragging them.

167

6 Tap once on the **Split** option in Step 3 to split the video clip at the point of the Playhead. Tap on the button between the two clips

7 Select a transition effect here which will appear between the two video clips

Use these buttons on the bottom toolbar to, from left to right, view the audio timeline and undo editing actions.

Working with Video Projects

Once a video project has been completed it can be managed on the iMovie Home screen. To do this:

1 Tap once on this button once a video project has been completed

Don't forget

The thumbnail used to depict a video project is taken from the first frame of the project.

2 All video projects are displayed here

Hot tip

Tap once on this arrow in the top left-hand corner of any iMovie screen to move back up one level.

3 Tap once on a video project to view its details

4 Tap once on the project's name and enter a new name for it. Tap on the **Done** button on the keyboard

5 The new name is displayed on the project's thumbnail

6 Tap once on this button to play the project

7 Tap once on this button to delete the project

8 Tap once on this button to edit the project

9 Select a project and tap once on this button to share it to a variety of locations

Hot tip

The **Theater** area displays items that have been shared via iCloud. This can be used to view all of your iCloud video content. Videos can be downloaded from iCloud by tapping once on this button in the Theater.

Viewing Videos

As the name suggests, the Videos app can be used to download and view video content. This is from the iTunes Store, rather than viewing your own videos. To do this:

Don't forget

If you rent videos from the iTunes Store you have to watch them within 30 days. Once you have started watching the video you have to finish watching it within 48 hours. Once the rental period has expired, the video is deleted from your iPad.

170

Beware

Videos can take up a lot of storage space once they are downloaded to your iPad.

Hot tip

You can also watch videos on a large screen HDTV, by connecting your iPad with an Apple Lightning Digital AV Adapter, which is sold separately.

1 Tap once on the **Videos** app

2 The Videos app is initially empty of content. Tap once on the **Store** button to access video content in the **iTunes Store**

3 Tap once on the **Films** button or the **TV** button

4 Tap once on an item to review its content. Tap once here to download it. This is usually in the form of buying or renting a video

5 The downloaded video appears in the Videos app. Tap once on the cover to view its contents

6 Tap once here to play a video

8 Music, Games and More

For entertainment the iPad is hard to beat. Games and music are the staple of many children and this chapter shows how they can make the most of them.

Using iTunes Store

Music on the iPad can be downloaded and played using the iTunes and the Music apps respectively. iTunes links to the iTunes Store, from where music, and other content, can be bought and downloaded to your iPad. To do this:

The Genius function is one where iTunes suggests songs and albums based on your previous purchases. If you have iTunes on a desktop or laptop computer you can turn on Genius to improve the options that appear on the iPad. To do this, select **Store > Turn on Genius** from the iTunes menu bar.

1 Tap once on this icon

2 Tap once on the **Music** button on the iTunes toolbar at the bottom of the window

3 Use these buttons at the top of the window to find music

4 Tap once on an item to view it. Tap once here to buy an album or tap on the button next to a song to buy that individual song

5 Purchased items are included in the Music app's Library

Playing Music

Once music has been bought on iTunes it can be played on your iPad using the Music app. To do this:

1 Tap once on this icon

2 Use these buttons to find songs by different criteria

3 Tap once on a track to select it and start it playing

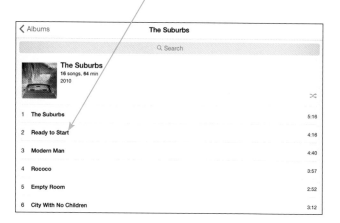

4 Tap once on the middle button to pause/play a selected song

5 Drag this button to increase or decrease the volume

6 Tap once on this button to repeat a song or album after it has played

Repeat

7 Tap once on this button to shuffle the order of songs (for an album or playlist)

Shuffle

Beware

When your child is listening to any music on the iPad, particularly with headphones, make sure that the sound level is not too high, so as not to damage hearing.

Don't forget

Playlists of specific songs can also be created within the Music app. To do this, tap once on the **Playlist** button on the bottom toolbar. Then tap once on the **New Playlist** button, give it a name and add songs from the Music Library. Once a playlist has been created it can be accessed from the **Playlist** button again.

...cont'd

Full cover view

Cover artwork for songs and albums can be viewed at full-screen size while the songs are being played. You can also view a track list in this view. To do this:

1 While a song is being played, tap once on this button

2 Tap once on the album cover to show or hide the toolbars

3 Use the music controls to manage tracks and tap on this button to view full details of an album

4 Tap once on a track to play it

5 Tap once on the **Done** button to go back up one level

Creating Music

For any children who are musically inclined there are several apps for creating music on the iPad. One of the most popular is Apple's GarageBand, which is an iPad app (from the App Store) of the full desktop/laptop version which is contained in the Mac iLife suite. GarageBand enables you to create music with a variety of digital instruments and also includes pre-recorded loops. To create music with GarageBand:

1 Tap once on this icon

2 Tap once on an instrument to select it as an input device

3 Tap once on the instrument button to access additional options

4 Tap once on the red **Record** button and play the instrument to create music with it

There are other music-making apps in the App Store and also apps to enhance GarageBand.

Swipe left and right to access the different instruments that are available in GarageBand.

Tap once on this button to stop recording.

...cont'd

Hot tip

Double-tap on a track icon to add more content to it with the same instrument.

Don't forget

Tap once on these buttons to move between the instrument input options and the main track list.

Hot tip

One of the instrument options is for plugging in a guitar amp, which is done with the headphone jack. This enables an electric guitar to be played directly onto a track.

5 The track is placed in the main window

6 Tap once on the **Instruments** button or tap once on this button in the bottom left-hand corner to access the instruments again and record another track

7 Individual tracks are placed underneath each other

8 Tap once on the track icon to access the **Delete, Duplicate, Rename** or **Merge** buttons

9 Swipe this button to show or hide the track controls

10 Use these buttons to, from left to right, go to the start of a project, play a project, record a track and adjust the volume for a track

GarageBand settings

There are options at the right-hand side of the main toolbar for adding pre-recorded loops of music and general settings:

1 Tap once on this button to access the pre-recorded loops of music

When a suitable loop has been identified it can be added to a song by dragging it onto the main track window.

2 Tap once on the **Instrument** link above to access options for loops created with different instruments

3 Tap once on this button to select settings for a selected track

4 Tap once on this button to select general settings for GarageBand

If the Metronome is turned **On** it will play a rhythm when an instrument is being recorded for a track.

177

...cont'd

Editing tracks

Once tracks have been created they can then be edited in a number of ways. To do this:

Don't forget

If a track is looped, it will be repeated once immediately after the selected area.

1 Tap once on a track so that a thick border, with a button at the end, appears

2 Drag on the button to trim the length of the track

Hot tip

If you select **Split**, a scissors icon appears. Drag this to the point where you want to split the track. Swipe down on the scissors to split the track. The different segments can then be edited separately.

3 Double-tap on a track to access its menu bar. Use this to **Cut**, **Copy**, **Paste**, **Delete**, **Trim**, **Split**, **Edit** or **Rename** the track

Managing projects

Once projects have been created they can then be managed in the My Songs area. To do this:

1 When you have finished creating or editing a song, tap once on this button

2 Completed projects appear here. Tap once on the name to overwrite it with a new one. Swipe left or right to move between projects

Tap once on a selected song in **My Songs** to open it for editing. Tap once on this button to create a new song.

179

3 Tap once on the **Select** button and tap once on a song to select it for management options

4 Tap once on this button to share the selected song via sites including Facebook and YouTube

5 Tap once on this button to duplicate the selected song

6 Tap once on this button to delete the selected song

7 Tap once on this button to save the selected song to iCloud

8 Tap once on the **Done** button to complete the actions that have been selected

Playing Games

Computer games are definitely an area where children can be considered experts and they will generally be able to guide adults in terms of obtaining the best games and how to use them. On the iPad there are two main avenues for playing games:

- Through the in-built Game Center app

- With games directly from the App Store

However, parents and teachers should still take a keen interest in games on the iPad and their main areas of concern are:

- Ensuring that children do not spend too long playing games on the iPad at the expense of other activities. This comes down to parental control and the best way is to agree an amount of time that can be spent playing games. There has to be a certain amount of trust involved with this and open discussion is the best way to deal with it rather than turning it into an area of conflict. However, it should also be remembered that there are benefits in playing games, such as hand-eye coordination, concentration, problem solving and social interaction (with multiplayer games).

- Ensuring that children do not access inappropriate content by obtaining games that are not suitable for their age group. Restrictions for this can be put in place within the General section of the Settings app, where age levels can be set for downloading apps (see Chapter Three for details about this).

Within both the Game Center and the App Store there are games for all ages, covering a variety of areas:

- Action

- Adventure

- Arcade

- Puzzles

- Racing

- Role Playing

- Sports

Hot tip

For a lot of games, there are 'cheats' that can be found on the Web. These are tips and shortcuts about achieving higher scores and overcoming particularly difficult obstacles. Children are usually well versed in finding these, frequently through word of mouth from their peers.

Game Center

The Game Center is a built-in iPad app for obtaining and playing games. It can also be used to play games with other people and rate your scores against other Game Center users.
To use the Game Center:

When you first open the Game Center you will have to sign-in with your Apple ID and give yourself a Game Center name that will be visible to other Game Center users.

1 Tap once on this icon

2 Tap once on the **Me** button and select options from the bubbles

3 Swipe up the **Me** screen to view game recommendations. Tap on one to view a preview and download it

The Game Center games are part of the main App Store and can be downloaded directly from there too.

...cont'd

4 Tap once on the **Games** button to view your games on the iPad and any compatible iOS devices

5 Tap once on a game to view details about it, such as the high scores of other players

6 Tap once on the **Friends** button. Tap here to invite friends to your Game Center, so that you can compare

games and scores. Also, for some games, you can play against your friends

Beware

Only accept requests from other Game Center users who you know. Never accept a request from a stranger. Don't forget to advise your children to follow the same rule.

App Store Games

A wide range of games is available in the App Store. These cover a variety of types and also different age groups. To access games:

1 Access the App Store and tap once on the **Games** button

2 The latest featured games are shown in the top panel and others are shown below. Swipe left and right to view more games

3 Swipe up and down to view currently-popular games and recommendations

A lot of games that are free to purchase then have offers of items within the game that need to be purchased. These are known as In-App purchases. If you do not want this to be possible, it can be turned off within the **Restrictions** area of the **General** section of the **Settings** app. See Chapter Three for more details about restrictions.

4 Tap once on a game to preview it. Download it in the same way as for any other app

...cont'd

Some to try

Choosing games can be very subjective but children are well equipped to find the ones that they like best, partly through word of mouth from their peers. However, here are a few games that provide opportunities for a range of age groups:

- **Ace Rider.** A motorbike racing game with a daring stuntman

- **Angry Birds.** One of the top iPad games, involving the angry birds trying to destroy greedy pigs

- **DragonVale.** For younger children, a role-playing game where you have to raise and breed your own dragons

- **Grand Theft Auto.** One of the most popular games in computing history, featuring the activities in Liberty City

- **Jelly Splash.** Another game for younger children, which involves connecting jelly symbols to complete levels

- **Kingdom Rush.** A fantasy defence game where you have to protect your kingdom against orcs, trolls, wizards and more

- **NFL Quarterback 13.** For any fans of American football

- **Peppa Pig's Party Time.** Play party games with this game featuring the popular cartoon character

- **Quell.** A puzzle game suitable for most ages where you move around various screens, collecting pearls

- **Scrabble for iPad.** An iPad version of the popular word game

- **Sliding Tiles.** An educational game consisting of puzzles where you move pieces to complete various tasks

- **Tap Pet Shop.** Create your own pet shop and look after animals so that customers can adopt them

- **Temple Run.** A simple but addictive game where you have to run as far as you can through a temple of obstacles

- **Tiny Zoo Friends.** A simulation game for younger children to collect, and care for, zoo animals

- **Where's My Water.** A series of puzzles that stress the environmental importance of preserving water

Drawing and Painting Apps

When famous artists start using painting and drawing apps on the iPad you know that this is a serious option for creating pictures. The artist David Hockney is a well known exponent of the iPad and has produced some stunning artwork with it. Even if you are not an internationally renowned artist, there are some great options for drawing and painting on the iPad. This can be done just for pleasure, or they can be used to produce diagrams for school work. To use drawing and painting apps (these examples are for the Drawing Pad app, but the functionality is similar for most drawing and painting apps):

1 Tap on one of the options on the main menu. Tap once on **New** to create a new painting

Don't forget

David Hockney uses the Brushes app for creating his artwork.

185

2 Tap once on one of the drawing or painting tools

3 The full range for a tool is displayed. Tap once to select a tool

4 Swipe left and right to move between the available tools

...cont'd

5 Drag on the screen to create a picture

6 Tap once on the **Save** option to access options for saving, printing and sharing the picture

---

Hot tip

If you want to hide the main toolbar in drawing and painting apps, to give you more space for your picture, this can usually be done by swiping on the button at the top of the toolbar.

---

7 Tap once on the **Menu** button to return to the Home screen at any time

8 Tap once on the **Album** button to view the pictures that have been created

9 Communicating

This chapter shows how to enhance your digital experience by getting online with the Safari web browser and communicating with email, messaging and connecting to social media.

Getting Connected

Accessing the Internet is a key part of communication on the iPad. Not only does it provide access to the Web and email, it also ensures connection to the App Store and apps including iTunes, Videos and Maps. iPads connect to the Internet via Wi-Fi: if it is in the home it will connect to this automatically once it has been set up; if it is in a public Wi-Fi area it will ask which network you would like to join. To connect to a Wi-Fi network:

Don't forget

When you enter a password for a Wi-Fi router, you can also use the **Join** button on the iPad keyboard.

1 Tap once on this icon

2 Tap once on the **Wi-Fi** link

3 Ensure the Wi-Fi button is in the **On** position

4 Available networks are shown here. Tap once on a network to select it

Beware

If a padlock appears next to a network it indicates it is a secure network, i.e. one that requires a password before you can join it. If there is no padlock it is unsecured which means that it could be easier for other people to hack into your iPad, if they are that way inclined. However, it is still unlikely to happen.

5 Enter a password for your Wi-Fi router and tap once on the **Join** button

6 Once a network has been joined, a tick appears next to it. This now provides access to the Internet

Using Safari

The Safari app is the default web browser on the iPad. This can be used to view web pages, save favorites and read pages with the Reader function. To use Safari:

1 Tap once on this icon

2 Tap once on the Address Bar and type a web page address. Suggested options appear as you type

3 Tap once on the **Go** button on the keyboard to open the web page

4 The selected web page opens in Safari. Swipe up and down and left and right to navigate around the page

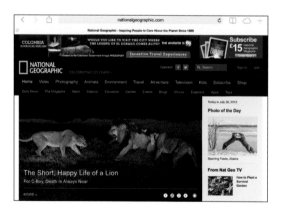

5 Tap once on the **Share** button to access options for bookmarking a page, adding it to the reading list to view at a later time, adding an icon to the Home screen for quick access to the page, emailing or tweeting the link for the page, and printing it

There are other browser apps for the iPad, including Chrome, Atomic, Opera, Mercury Skyfire and Dolphin. There is also Mobicip Safe Browser which can restrict certain types of content (see page 59).

Double-tap with one finger on a web page to zoom in on it. Double-tap again to return to normal view.

Safari Settings (**Settings > Safari**) can be used for a selection of items including privacy and security and settings for tabs and blocking pop-ups.

Navigating Pages

When you are viewing pages within Safari there are a number of functions that can be used:

Hot tip

The Reading List can be used for pages that you want to read later, and when you are offline. Shared Links shows links from Twitter, if you have linked your iPad to a Twitter account.

Hot tip

If a web page has this button in the Address/ Search box it means that the page can be viewed with the **Reader** function. This displays the page as text only, without any of the accompanying design to distract from the content. Tap on the button so that it turns black to activate the Reader.

1 Tap once on these buttons to move forward and back between web pages that have been visited

2 Tap once here to view Bookmarked pages, Reading List pages and Shared Links

3 Tap once here to add a bookmark, add to a reading list, add an icon to your iPad Home screen, email a link to a page, tweet a page, send it to Facebook or print a page

4 Tap once here to add a new tab

5 Tap once on a link on a page to open it. Tap and hold to access additional options, to open in a new tab, add to a Reading List or copy the link

6 Tap and hold on an image and tap once on **Save Image** or **Copy**

Opening New Tabs

Safari supports tabbed browsing, which means that you can open separate pages within the same window and access them by tapping on each tab at the top of the page:

1 Tap once here to open a new tab for another page

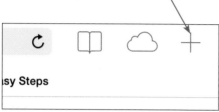

2 Open a new page by entering a web address into the Address Bar, or tap on one of the thumbnails in the **Favorites** window

3 Tap once on the tab headings to move between tabbed pages

4 Tap once on the cross at the top of a tab to close it

Email on the iPad

Email on the iPad is sent and received using the Mail app. This provides a range of functionality for managing email. To use this:

1 Tap once on this icon (the red icon in the corner displays the number of unread emails)

2 Tap once on a message to display it in the main panel

You can also save an image in an email by pressing and holding on it and tapping once on the **Save Image** button. This also gives you an option for copying the image so that you can paste it elsewhere.

3 Use these buttons to, from left to right: flag, move, delete, respond and create a new message

4 Tap once on this button and then Reply to a message, Forward it to a new recipient, Save an Image in a message or Print it

5 Tap once on this button to create a new message

6 Enter a recipient, subject and body text. Tap once on the **Send** button

Subject: Lunch tomorrow?

Hi, would you like to have lunch tomorrow?

Sent from my iPad

Mailboxes

Different categories of email messages can be managed via mailboxes. For instance, your child may want to keep their social emails separately from ones that apply to school activities. To use different mailboxes:

1 From your Inbox, tap once on the **Mailboxes** button

2 The current mailboxes are displayed. Tap once on the **Edit** button

3 Tap once on the **New Mailbox** button at the bottom of the Mailboxes panel

New Mailbox

4 Enter a name for the new mailbox and tap once on the **Save** button

5 Tap once on the **Done** button

Done

6 To delete a mailbox, tap on it once at Step 3, instead of the New Mailbox button, and tap on the **Delete Mailbox** button

...cont'd

Email threads

When you receive a number of emails on the same subject, they can be sorted into threads, for easier viewing. To do this:

The Threads function can be turned **On** and **Off** in the **Settings** app under the **Mail, Contacts, Calendars** link. In the **Mail** section, drag the **Organize by Thread** button **On** or **Off**.

1 If there is an email thread, you will see this symbol next to the top email

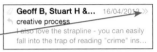

2 Tap on this symbol next to the email to view the items in the full thread

3 Tap once on an individual email in the thread to view its contents

Editing Mailboxes

Messages can be edited within individual mailboxes. To do this:

Individual emails can also be deleted from mailboxes by swiping on them from right to left and tapping on the **Trash** button.

1 Tap once on a mailbox

2 Tap once on the **Edit** button

3 Tap once next to a message to select it and tap once on one of the **Mark**, **Move** or **Trash** options at the bottom of the panel

Email settings and accounts

Email settings can be specified within the Settings app. Different email accounts can also be added here.

1 Tap once on this icon

2 Tap once on the **Mail, Contacts, Calendars** link

3 Under the Mail section there are several options for how Mail operates and looks. These include the number of messages being displayed, previewing emails and font size

4 Tap once on the **Add Account** link to add a new account

5 Tap once on the type of email account you want to add

6 Enter the details for the account. Tap once on the **Next** button to complete the account setup process

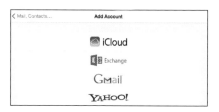

Hot tip

One of the Mail settings is for changing the email signature, i.e. the message that appears automatically at the bottom of each email. By default it says **Sent from my iPad**. To change this, tap once on the **Signature** link and type a new signature message.

Messaging

Text messaging is one of the favorite pastimes of the younger generation, on any device that is to hand for the purpose. On your iPad you can join the world of text with the Apple iMessage service that is accessed via the Messages app. This enables text and photo messages to be sent, free of charge, between users of the iOS 5 to iOS 7 operating systems on the iPad, iPhone and iPod Touch, and Mac computers with OS X Mountain Lion or a later version of the Mac operating system. iMessages can be sent to cell/mobile phone numbers and email addresses. To use iMessages:

1 Tap once on the **Messages** app

2 Enter your Apple ID details and tap once on the **Sign in** button

Beware

If a number, or an email address, is not recognized it shows up in red in the **To** box.

3 Tap once on this button to create a new message and start a new conversation

4 Tap once on this button to select someone from your contacts

5 Tap once on a contact to select them as the recipient of the new message

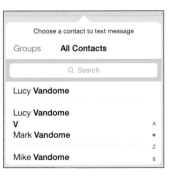

Creating iMessages

To create and edit messages and conversations:

1 Tap once here and type with the keyboard to create a message. Tap once on the **Send** button

2 As the conversation progresses each message is displayed here

Hot tip

Press and hold on a message and tap on the **More** button that appears. Select a message and tap on the **Trash** icon to remove it.

197

3 To edit whole conversations, tap once on the **Edit** button in the Messages panel

Edit

Don't forget

When a message has been sent you are notified underneath it if it has been delivered.

4 Tap once here and tap once on the **Delete** button to delete the conversation

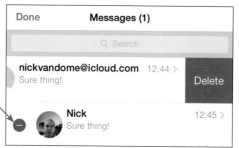

Social Networking

Young people have always found ways to interact with their peers and the Internet has now provided a virtual means to do this through social networking sites. These are websites and text messaging services that link people so that they can share information, photos, thoughts, opinions, jokes and almost anything else that they want to. Facebook and Twitter have been two of the main players in this area but, as they have become more mainstream, young people are also looking at new sites for their social networking.

Facebook

Despite the range of new sites this is still one of the most widely-used social networking tools. To use Facebook you have to first register, which is free. You can then link up with your friends by searching for them and inviting them with a Friend Request. You can also be invited by other people and you have to accept their request before you can be friends. The types of things you can do on Facebook are:

- Posting of status messages – telling the world what you have been doing or your opinions about things

- Adding photos

- Commenting on your friends' posts and photos

- Private messaging. Sending private messages to your friends

- Creating and joining groups of people with similar interests and hobbies

Facebook can be accessed on your iPad through their website on Safari. However, there is also a Facebook app that can be downloaded from the App Store which is designed for mobile access to Facebook. You can also install the Facebook app and create an account from the **Settings** app.

See Chapter Three for details about security issues on social networking sites.

Search for 'In Easy Steps' in Facebook and you'll be taken to the In Easy Steps Facebook page. If you click on **Like** and then under **Liked**, click on **Get Notifications** you'll automatically get updates on new titles, etc.

198

Most young people use several different social networking sites and do not limit themselves to just one or two.

Twitter

Twitter is a relatively well-established social networking tool, launched in 2006, but it has grown at a remarkable rate and is now one of the most visited websites in the world. It is a microblogging site where users post short messages, of up to 140 characters. Once you have joined Twitter you can follow other users to see what they are saying and have people follow you too. To use Twitter on your iPad:

You can follow In Easy Steps on Twitter (@InEasySteps).

1 Tap once on this icon

2 Tap once on the **Twitter** link

3 Tap once on the **Install** button to install the Twitter app

A message on Twitter is known as a tweet.

4 Enter the required account details and tap once on the **Sign In** button

User Name	@nickvandome
Password	••••••••
Sign In	
Create New Account	

5 In the Twitter Settings, tap once on the **Create New Account** button

6 Tap once on this icon to access Twitter through the iPad Twitter app

...cont'd

Snapchat

Launched in 2011, Snapchat has quickly caught the imagination of social networking users. It is a messaging service that allows users to send photos and videos to their Snapchat friends. Once these are accessed they remain visible for up to 10 seconds and then they are deleted. Text and graphics can be added to items when they are sent and one of the most frequent uses is for sending self-portraits (selfies).

One of the downsides of Snapchat is the potential for inappropriate material to be sent, on the basis that it will be deleted after the user has viewed it. However, there are ways in which images can be saved before they are deleted, so great care should still be exercised in terms of the type of content that is sent via Snapchat.

Google+

This is Google's answer to Facebook. It allows users to create Circles of friends and people can be added in a similar way as adding Friends on Facebook. Different content can be shared with each Circle that is created. You need to have a Google account to use Google+ and there is also a function for video messaging, called Hangouts. For teenagers, the popularity of Google+ could be hindered by the fact that it is linked to such a mainstream company, but there are a range of security measures on the site that add to its appeal.

Instagram

This is a popular photo and video sharing site. Followers can be added for users and they can then comment and 'like' photos. By default, the security settings are for public viewing of content, so these should be changed if you only want your own followers to be able to view your content.

Tumblr

This combines the functions of a number of other sites and can be used like an online diary, where you post your photos, videos and own thoughts and ideas in a series of blogs. These are known as Tumblelogs and can be viewed by your Tumblr contacts, or everyone if the account is public. If you have Facebook and Twitter accounts your Tumblr content can also be linked to these. It can be harder to make your account private on Tumblr than on some other sites.

Don't forget

The combination of young people and social networking means that new products are being developed and experimented with at a rapid rate. Sites fall in and out of fashion so it can be hard to keep up with what is the latest 'in' thing (those listed here are just a small selection of what is available). But, in general, the same rules apply for all of these sites: talk to your children about them, make sure they are not interacting with people they don't know, that they are not being bullied online and that they are not posting, or looking at, inappropriate material.

Using FaceTime

Video chatting is a very personal and interactive way to keep in touch with family and friends around the world. The FaceTime app provides this facility with other iOS 5, iOS 6 and iOS 7 users on the iPad, iPhone and iPod Touch, or a Mac computer with FaceTime. To use FaceTime for video chatting:

1 Tap once on the **FaceTime** app

FaceTime has to be turned on in the **FaceTime** section of the **Settings** app.

2 Sign in using your Apple ID to create your FaceTime account

3 Tap once on the **Contacts** button

4 Tap once on a contact to access their details for making a FaceTime call

5 Tap once on their phone number or email address to make a FaceTime call. The recipient must have FaceTime on their iPad, iPhone, iPod Touch or Mac computer

6 Tap once on the **Add to Favorites** button to add the contact to your favorites list, for quick access

Add to Favorites

...cont'd

7 Once you have selected a contact, FaceTime starts connecting to them and displays this button

8 When you have connected, your contact appears in the main window and you appear in a picture-in-picture thumbnail in the corner

9 Tap once on this button to swap between cameras on your iPad

10 Tap once on this button to end the FaceTime call

 End

11 If someone else makes a call to you, tap once on the **Decline** or **Accept** buttons

10 Sharing with the iPad

This chapter shows how to back up, transfer and share files on your iPad.

Using iCloud

iCloud is the Apple service for storing and backing up items on your iPad. It can also be used to make photos, videos, music, settings and data available across other iCloud-enabled devices, including other iPads, iPhones, iPod Touches (with iOS 5 or later) and iMacs and MacBooks (with OS X Lion or later installed).

When your iPad is connected to the Internet over Wi-Fi, iCloud will back up the following items automatically if the iPad is connected to a power source and is locked:

- Purchased music, TV shows, apps and books

- Photos

- Settings and app data

With an iCloud account you get a free email account and 5GB of storage for documents and backup. (*Correct at the time of printing.*) You can also purchase extra storage if required.

Once iCloud has been set up it takes care of all of the saving, backing up and synchronizing issues for the selected content. You then access this content from any iCloud-enabled device.

iCloud Settings
To set up iCloud:

Beware

iCloud only backs up music purchased from iTunes. If you have imported any of your own music via iTunes this will not be backed up.

Hot tip

Your iCloud account can be accessed online from any Internet-enabled computer at www.icloud.com

1   Tap once on this icon

2   Tap once on the **iCloud** link

3   Enter your Apple ID details, if you have one, or tap on the **Get a Free Apple ID** button. These details can then be used to set up iCloud

4 Drag these buttons to the **On** position for all of the items you would like to include in iCloud. These items will be backed up automatically by iCloud

5 Tap once on the **Photos** link above and drag the **My Photo Stream** button to **On** so iCloud will copy your photos and make them available to other compatible devices

6 Tap once on the **Documents & Data** link and drag the button to **On** to copy your documents to iCloud

7 Tap once on the **Storage & Backup** link

8 Tap once on the **Change Storage Plan** link to view how your storage is being used and add more if required

Tap once on the **Change Storage Plan** link to upgrade your iCloud storage. Above 5GB there is a charge, depending on how much storage you require.

Backing up with iCloud

Not only can iCloud store the content from your iPad and make it available to other devices, it can also back it up in case it is deleted or your iPad is lost or destroyed. Data stored on iCloud can then be restored, either to your original iPad, or even a new device. To back up with iCloud:

1 Access the iCloud section of the Settings app and tap once on the **Storage & Backup** link

2 Drag the **iCloud Backup** button to **On**

Beware

If you want to test the restore process you can do so by resetting your iPad under the **General** section of the **Settings** app, by tapping once on the **Reset** link and then **Erase All Content and Settings**. However, if there is no need to do it then it is best not to.

3 Tap once on the **Back Up Now** link. iCloud will then back up your data automatically when it is has an online connection via Wi-Fi. The latest backup is shown underneath the Back Up Now link

Back Up Now

Last Backup: 19:36

4 If you ever need to restore the data to your iPad, or to another device, restart the device and tap once on the **Restore from iCloud Backup** link during the setup process (this is the same as the setup process for when you first start using your iPad) rather than the **Set Up as New iPad** link. This will then restore all of the data from the iCloud backup

Managing Storage

When you are backing up the content on your iPad to iCloud you can specify manually which items are included in the backup. This is done in the Storage & Backup section as shown on the previous page. To manage your iCloud storage:

1 In **Storage & Backup** section, tap once on the **Manage Storage** link

STORAGE	
Total Storage	25.0 GB
Available	23.0 GB
Manage Storage	>

2 Tap once on your iPad's name in the **Backups** section. (Underneath this there are details of iWork apps that store documents and data in iCloud. Tap once on each to see what specific files are being stored)

3 Backup details are displayed at the top of the window, underneath the iPad's name. Drag these buttons **On** or **Off** to include, or exclude, apps in the iCloud backup. If they are dragged **Off**, any previously-backed up data will be deleted

If you select the **Delete Backup** button in Step 3 this will delete all of the information that has been previously backed up to iCloud. It is not recommended that this is done, unless you have a good reason to do so.

Sharing with iTunes

Items on your iPad can be shared via other computers using iTunes. This can include synchronizing music, movies, books, photos and apps. You can also share documents that you have created on your iPad, if the other computer has compatible apps for viewing and editing them.

Syncing with iTunes

Synchronization with your iPad and iTunes can either be done over Wi-Fi or with the USB Lightning Connector cable that comes with the iPad. To do this:

Beware

Music and photos can take up a lot of storage space and could quickly fill up your iPad if you sync them from another computer. For both of these options you can select just to sync selected items, rather than your entire music or photo libraries. This is done in the panels for each item.

Hot tip

To sync over Wi-Fi, scroll down in the **Summary** panel. Under **Options**, check on the **Sync with this iPad over Wi-Fi** box.

1 Connect the iPad to the other computer and open iTunes on that computer

2 The iPad shows up in the **Devices** panel of iTunes

3 Set up the iPad ready for synchronizing. Select any items you want synced automatically

4 The Summary panel displays general information about the iPad

5 Tap once on the main toolbar to select the items that you want to sync

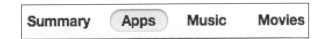

6   Tap once next to the items you want to sync

7   Tap once on the **Sync** button

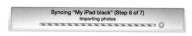

8   The progress of the synchronization is displayed at the top of the iTunes window

An iPad can be synced with iTunes on either a Mac computer or a Windows one.

Transferring files

Files can be transferred from your iPad to another computer, and vice versa, using iTunes. First, you have to save the iPad files to iTunes and then you can transfer them to compatible apps on another computer with iTunes. To do this:

1   In an appropriate app, tap once on the tools button and tap once on the **Send a copy** link

2   Tap once on the **iTunes** link

Transferring documents as PDF files is a good option for allowing them to be viewed on other computers. However, for editing purposes it is best to save them in a format that is compatible with an app on the other computer, so that they can be opened and changed.

3   Select a format in which you want to transfer the document

...cont'd

Don't forget

In order to share documents with iTunes, the app has to support this function. Check an app's Help file (if it has one) to see whether it supports iTunes sharing.

Hot tip

Photos and videos can be transferred to a Windows PC by connecting with the Lightning cable connector and accessing the iPad through File Explorer and then copying and pasting the required files.

4 Connect your iPad to a computer and open iTunes. Tap once on the **Apps** button on the top toolbar

5 Scroll down to the File Sharing section and select an app

6 Tap once on a document

7 Tap once on **Save to...** button and select a location on your computer where you would like to save the document

Save to...

8 Tap once on **Add...** button to select a file and add it to the iPad

Add...

9 In an app on the iPad, tap here in the Documents section and select **Copy from iTunes**, to open a document that has been copied from another computer with iTunes

| Create Document | + |
| Copy from iTunes | ♫ |

10 Tap once on the document that you want to copy

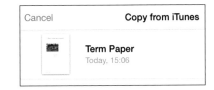

Index

Q

R

S

T

U

V

W

Z